Advance
The World Is \
Celebrating the 50th Ordinati... ...iversary of Addie Davis

This is a remarkable collection of sermons, from Addie Davis' pioneering work in the '60s to the stellar contributions of recent seminary graduates. The Baptist world has been needing these voices for a long time, and thankfully these are women who could not wait to proclaim the Gospel. They offer a more comprehensive view of God, who has been urging them to speak all along.

—Molly T. Marshall
President
Central Baptist Theological Seminary
Shawnee, Kansas

Hope for the church and the world is alive and well in the words of these gifted women. Keen insight, delightful observations, profound courage, and a gift for communicating the good news are woven throughout these sermons. The Spirit so evident in Addie Davis' life and calling clearly continues in her legacy.

—Dorisanne Cooper
Pastor
Watts Street Baptist Church
Durham, North Carolina

The words of these preachers are true to the Spirit of Christ and a sense of calling that comes from God's heart to theirs. I celebrate the gifts these sermons will release in the lives of the people who read them. It is an honor and joy to recommend *The World is Waiting for You.*

—J. Truett Gannon
Professor Emeritus of Ministry Experience
McAfee School of Theology
Mercer University
Atlanta, Georgia

In the words of Addie Davis, "the frontier is limitless in the realm of God's spirit." This exceptional compilation of sermons and reflections points us to the horizon of our shared future, ringing with the songs from a choir of dynamic, colorful, and faithful women. For just as they resound with resurrection hope, so too might we all feel the unbridled possibility of God's spirit of Love at work among us!

—**Emily Hull McGee**
Minister to Young Adults
Highland Baptist Church
Louisville, Kentucky

Half a century removed from the ordination of Addie Davis, there are still so many preaching voices we need to hear. I'm grateful for a book that amplifies some of them for us.

—**Alan Sherouse**
Pastor
First Baptist Church
Greensboro, North Carolina

THE WORLD IS WAITING FOR YOU

Smyth & Helwys Publishing, Inc.
6316 Peake Road
Macon, Georgia 31210-3960
1-800-747-3016
©2014 by Pamela R. Durso and LeAnn Gunter Johns
All rights reserved.

Library of Congress Cataloging-in-Publication Data

The world is waiting for you : celebrating the 50th ordination anniversary of
Addie Davis / edited by Pamela R. Durso and LeAnn Gunter Johns
pages cm
ISBN 978-1-57312-732-5 (pbk. : alk. paper)
1. Baptists--Sermons. 2. Sermons, American--Women authors.
I. Durso, Pamela R., editor of compilation.
BX6333.A1W67 2014
252'.061--dc23

2014016469

Disclaimer of Liability: With respect to statements of opinion or fact available in this work of nonfiction, Smyth & Helwys Publishing Inc. nor any of its employees, makes any warranty, express or implied, or assumes any legal liability or responsibility for the accuracy or completeness of any information disclosed, or represents that its use would not infringe privately-owned rights.

Edited By Pamela R. Durso & LeAnn Gunter Johns

The World

IS

WAITING

for You

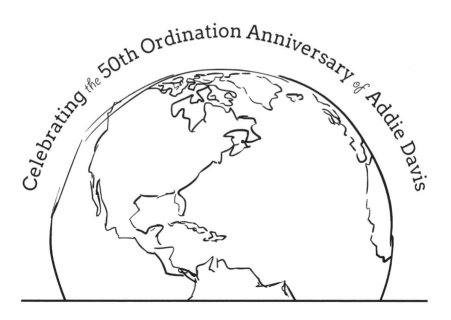

Celebrating the 50th Ordination Anniversary of Addie Davis

This book is dedicated to Addie Davis,
who blazed the trail on which so many of us now walk,

and to the many Baptist women
who have heard and followed God's calling,
even when it took them to hard places,

and to the girls and young women
who have yet to hear God's call.

The world needs what they have to offer.
We are waiting, God is waiting for them!

Contents

Preface

Pamela R. Durso and LeAnn Gunter Johns

Take a preacher and her writer friend, add in a publisher friend, throw in three cups of coffee, and suddenly there is a book idea. What began as an innocent conversation over coffee back in 2011 soon resulted in a book contract, which then became a collecting and writing project that finally evolved into the book you hold.

The morning coffee was courtesy of Panera Bread, but the idea was courtesy of our friend, Keith Gammons, publisher and executive vice president of Smyth & Helwys Publishing. Our best memory is that he was the instigator of the conversation; he was the one who dreamed up the idea of pulling together a new book of sermons. (We think he may have paid for the coffee too.) Keith's initiation of a new joint project should not have been a surprise to either of us. For the last six years, he has been the dreamer behind a good number of Baptist Women in Ministry's best creations. Back in 2008, he had the lovely idea of publishing a book of sermons titled *This Is What a Preacher Looks Like* to go along with the T-Shirt that BWIM was selling at the time. In 2012, his decision to publish a devotional collection for BWIM's thirtieth-anniversary celebration resulted in the 2013 fall issue of Smyth & Helwys's *Reflections* being filled with the beautiful words of 122 supporters of BWIM. But Keith did not stop there. He invited BWIM to provide weekly devotionals for the new NextSunday Resources blog Coracle, and in January 2014, the first devotionals, written by Julie Pennington-Russell, were read and appreciated by hundreds of folks. And now, here in mid-2014, more evidence of this partnership has emerged, and Keith Gammons is once again responsible.

Keith's dream this time was to help BWIM to celebrate another special occasion—a fiftieth anniversary! This year, in 2014, we remember and give thanks for Addie Davis, who in 1964 became the first woman to be ordained by a Southern Baptist church. In August 1964, Watts Street Baptist Church in Durham, North Carolina, ordained her to the gospel ministry.

During the next forty years, Addie pastored three churches—one in Vermont, one in Rhode Island, and one in Virginia. Throughout those years, she was an inspiration to many of the women who followed her into ministry and were ordained. Addie was often invited to speak at women in ministry conferences, and her ordination became a well-celebrated milestone for the moderate and progressive Baptists who supported women in ministry. Despite the attention focused on her, Addie never seemed to understand the importance of her place in our history. As Diane Hill, minister of adults at Watts Street, noted, Addie's "focus was not on the cause of women in ministry but on ministry," and Addie spent her years as a pastor seeking to follow God's calling and to live fully and faithfully into that calling.[1]

Not surprisingly, Addie became a much loved and admired hero for Baptist Women in Ministry. Her willingness to "be the first" inspired that admiration, but her courage and humility proved to be the greater inspiration. In recognition and appreciation of her ministry, BWIM's leadership established the Addie Davis Awards in 1994, on the thirtieth anniversary of Addie's ordination. At the worship service that year, BWIM collected an offering to support the award, and four years later, in 1998, the first Addie Davis Awards were presented. Every year since 1998, award nominations have been gathered from the seminaries and theological schools affiliated with the Cooperative Baptist Fellowship. In 1998, all seven women nominated were given a preaching award. The next year, the BWIM board of directors voted to present awards to two individuals—one award for pastoral leadership and one for preaching. For sixteen years now, the Addie Davis Awards have been an attempt to honor an amazing woman but have also served as an affirmation of the gifts of all nominees and award recipients. On December 3, 2005, Addie Davis died, but through the BWIM awards, her legacy and encouragement live on.

Ten years ago, in June 2004, when I (LeAnn) was given the Addie Davis award for preaching, I had no idea the impact that it would have on my life and ministry. Having grown up in a Southern Baptist church, I had never seen a woman be ordained to the gospel ministry. On the day I received the award, I heard about Addie's ordination and ministry, and as a young woman who loved to preach, hearing her story encouraged me to continue following God's call on my life. Her courage in serving God when times were extremely difficult for a woman in ministry became an example of the risky faith that is required in vocational ministry. The award connected me to her. It also connected me to other women who have felt this call to preach, and who at some point have questioned where or how God would use their calling. I remain grateful for Addie Davis, and I am thankful that Baptist Women in Ministry continues to tell her story through this award each year.

Like me, each recipient has a different story of what the award has meant to her. Ellen Di Giosia, associate pastor of faith formation at Woodland Baptist Church in San Antonio, Texas, was the 2000 recipient of the Addie Davis Award for Outstanding Leadership in Pastoral Ministry. Her gratitude for the award has encouraged her to speak out of its importance in Baptist life: "I am so glad that BWIM has a way to help women feel affirmed in their calling and to give them a platform to speak to the larger Baptist community."[2]

The 2002 recipient of the Addie Davis Award for Excellence in Preaching, Andrea Dellinger Jones, is now pastor of Millbrook Baptist Church in Raleigh, North Carolina. When Andrea received the award, she realized that she was part of "a cloud of witnesses that verified talents in me that I wasn't even quite ready to affirm in myself. On difficult days in ministry and in times of doubt, the award gives me better footing to keep trying to do my best at this high and holy calling."[3]

Kyndall Rae Rothaus, the 2011 recipient of the Addie Davis Award for Excellence in Preaching, now serves as pastor of Covenant Baptist Church in San Antonio, Texas. For Kyndall, receiving the Addie Davis Award was like having somebody say, "Yes, you can be a preacher, despite your fears, despite your insecurities. You were meant for this. You can do this, and we're behind you. You're not alone."[4]

The 2012 recipient of the Addie Davis Award for Excellence in Preaching, Erin James-Brown, is now a chaplain at Texas Health Harris Methodist Hospital in Fort Worth, Texas. Of the award, Erin says, "A year after receiving the award I continue to feel the encouragement. I know that my gifts and talents are recognized as I continue to work and hone my skills, but because of the encouragement I've received I want to encourage others so that other women in ministry know that they have gifts and talents, creativity and love to share with others."[5]

The awards have preserved the beauty of Addie's life and have extended her legacy to the next generation of Baptist women ministers. We concluded that to celebrate the fiftieth anniversary of her ordination, there could be no more fitting and meaningful tribute than to produce a collection of sermons preached by Addie Davis Award recipients. This collection was the idea of Keith Gammons, but we quickly jumped on board. Over the past few years, together we gathered sermons, read those sermons, talked about those sermons, and read the sermons again, and we are convinced that this collection of beautiful and inspiring sermons from the award recipients is a perfect way to celebrate Addie's special anniversary.

The collection includes a biographical introduction to Addie as well as two of her sermons. The first of those sermons, "The Ministry of the Church," was the one she preached on August 30, 1964—her first Sunday at First Baptist Church of Readsboro, Vermont. The second sermon, "Waiting for You," was preached in Addie's home church, Covington Baptist Church, Covington, Virginia, on June 5, 1988.

Also included are sermons by eighteen recipients of the Addie Davis Awards—six recipients of the award for outstanding pastoral leadership and twelve recipients of the preaching award. Of the eighteen women, three are currently pastors, four serve on church staffs, four are chaplains, one is a homiletics professor, another is studying to be a homiletics professor, two are writers, one is a preacher who paints and creates music, and one is a writer who preaches as often as possible in the many places around the world where she has lived as a Navy spouse.

The final of the eighteen Addie Davis Award recipients is one dear to my (Pam's) heart: Gwen Brown. Gwen worked in the corporate world for many years, but in 2005, she suddenly found herself as pastor of a church. A Bible study meeting in her home blossomed into a church, and Gwen, in response to God's call to ministry, walked away from a successful career, enrolled at McAfee School of Theology, and gave herself fully to her new church. In 2010, the year Gwen graduated from McAfee, the BWIM leadership team presented her with the Addie Davis Award for Outstanding Leadership in Pastoral Ministry, and we were so impressed with and amazed by her giftedness that we quickly asked her to join our team. Gwen served BWIM brilliantly and became for us a voice of kindness and common sense, and in the midst of all that was unfolding with BWIM, a beautiful friendship developed. Gwen became my lunch partner and my fellow dreamer, and soon she also became my pastor. She first invited me to preach at Cornerstone Church. She then invited me to attend some of their special services. She kept inviting me, and I fell in love with Cornerstone. They became my family, my home, my church. Sadly, Gwen left us all too soon.

On August 27, 2013, after long months of illness, Gwen passed away, and one of God's best lights in this world was lost. In my grieving, I am discovering that, like Addie Davis, Gwen built a legacy that lives on—through Cornerstone and its continuing ministry, through the lives of so many young ministers whom she loved and mentored, and through her good words. I am thankful to include one of her sermons in this collection, and I am thankful to God for my dear friend, Gwen Brown.

As we read and pondered the words written by Gwen and the other seventeen preachers whose sermons are included in this book, we discovered that patterns emerged, offering a glimpse into the distinctiveness of women's preaching. While our findings are surely not scientifically based and are gleaned from only a small number of sermons, these observations may be helpful as we talk about and seek to understand the unique contributions of women in our pulpits.

Based on the sermons we received, we found that women preachers lean toward Gospel texts, and of all the Gospels, Luke seems to be the one favored by women. These findings are not surprising given that Jesus was an advocate for and friend to women and that Luke includes more stories about women than any of the other Gospels. We also discovered that a high percentage of the women preachers are narrative in their presentation style and that they often rely on everyday life stories in their sharing of the gospel message. We found that women preachers tend to be inviting and inclusive in their use of language—that is, they use the inclusive third person plural pronoun "we" rather than the more exclusive second person pronoun "you." By that seemingly simple word choice, women preachers invite their listeners into the story and ask them to be part of the experience. Finally, we discovered that these women preachers often tell personal stories. They connect to their listeners by sharing about themselves and their life experiences.

As you read the sermons in this collection, you may see other patterns, but you will also discover that each woman has a unique voice, her own sense of preaching style. No two women preachers are identical. Each woman has a beautiful, God-given gift of expression. In reading these sermons, you will also find that they were meant to be preached—spoken out loud in a congregational setting. The sermons were not originally intended for reading. Care has been taken to craft them into a readable format, but as is true for all good preaching, the preached word does not always translate exactly onto paper. Body language, facial expressions, and voice inflections cannot be captured in print. So as you read, imagine the preacher standing before you, her arms outstretched, her soothing voice, and her contagious energy and enthusiasm.

"Take a preacher and her writer friend, add in a publisher friend, throw in three cups of coffee, and suddenly there is a book idea." And then, suddenly (well, a little over two years later), there is a book. The key to the "suddenly" for us is the word "friend." Friendship has brought this book to completion. Our friendship goes back much farther than the two years that we have spent working on this project. BWIM actually introduced us to one another. We served together beginning in 2005 on the BWIM Leadership Team. LeAnn was a fresh-out-of-seminary minister, serving at Peachtree Baptist Church in Atlanta. Pam was a slightly older (okay, seventeen years older) Baptist historian/minister living in Nashville, Tennessee. After nine years, three moves (Pam to Atlanta, LeAnn to California and then to Macon, Georgia), two passed driver's license tests (by Pam's teenagers), two babies born (both to LeAnn), and thousands of hours talking on the phone and/or sitting over coffee, our friendship has become a stabilizing force in both our lives as well as a source of creativity and energy and a place to dream together. Given our friendship, creating a book together seemed a natural thing to undertake together. So when Keith Gammons put the book idea out on the table, we took him seriously, and "suddenly there is a book."

Working on a book with a friend has some side benefits—the best of which is that when a wonderful discovery is made, you have a co-author to call, someone who will get excited when you find a treasure. In searching through Addie Davis's papers that are archived at the Jack Tarver Library at Mercer University in Macon, we (meaning LeAnn) found what has become for us a treasure. That treasure was found in one of Addie's sermons. On June 5, 1988, she preached at her home church in Covington, Virginia. The church was celebrating the 100th anniversary of the Woman's Missionary Union (1888–1988) and recognizing recent high school graduates, and Addie's word to the young people in the congregation that day was "Remember that you are unique; God has made no two of us alike. And remember this is your day. Now is your turn. The world waits to see what you will do, and God waits expectantly for you."

In 1964, the world was waiting for Addie Davis. It was her day, her turn. Addie never seemed to understand her importance in our history, but her courage has given countless women encouragement to be brave in using their gifts for ministry. Each time a woman in ministry steps into a pulpit, enters a hospital room, or offers a prayer over a cup of coffee, she is living faithfully and fully into her calling from God. She, like Addie, may not see the importance of her ministry yet. She may not realize that it is her day, her turn. She may not know that the world is waiting for her and that God is waiting for her.

Our hope is that, through these awards that were named in her honor and given now in her memory, Addie's words will be heard by each award recipient, each nominee, and each and every woman called and gifted by God: "The world waits to see what you will do." Our prayer is that the Addie Davis awards will be an affirmation of the unique gifts, voices, and strengths of all women ministers—those now serving but especially those who have yet to hear God's call. The world needs what they have to offer. We are waiting for them, and God is waiting for them!

Notes

1. "Addie Davis, First Woman Ordained as Southern Baptist Pastor, Dies at 88," Associated Baptist Press, 9 December 2005.

2. In Pamela R. Durso and Amy Shorner-Johnson, "The State of Women in Baptist Life, 2010," commissioned by Baptist Women in Ministry, Atlanta GA, 2010, p. 3.

3. Ibid., 4.

4. "The 2013 Addie Davis Awards," video commissioned by Baptist Women in Ministry, Atlanta GA, 2013.

5. Ibid.

Remembering Addie

Pamela R. Durso

In this special year, 2014, we remember and give thanks for Addie Davis. Even though she is no longer with us, we celebrate this anniversary year. Fifty years ago, Addie became the first ordained woman minister in Southern Baptist circles when Watts Street Baptist Church in Durham, North Carolina, ordained her to the gospel ministry on August 9, 1964.

In the fifty years since that historic ordination, thousands of Baptist women called and gifted by God have been ordained, most of whom do not even know Addie's name even though they walk on the trail that she blazed. Addie's place in history makes her story extraordinary, but her own understanding of her life was that she was an ordinary person who sought to be faithful to God's call. Perhaps both interpretations of the life of Addie Davis are needed—she was truly an ordinary woman with experiences common to many other Baptists of her day. Even after her ordination and as she served for four decades in ministry, Addie lived quietly, doing the everyday tasks that every minister does. She never sought attention or looked for a larger platform for the cause of women in ministry. Instead, she found great contentment in routine pastoral duties like preaching, making hospital visits, talking with the children of the church, and making sure the church building was clean and well maintained—the ordinary stuff of ministry.

The extraordinary thing about Addie's story is that her faithfulness and persistence modeled for Baptists, especially for Baptist women, a new way of being and doing. Her willingness to follow God in a time when there were no role models, no support systems, and no encouragement of her call-ing in the South would soon become a source of inspiration for other women called by God. Although Addie died in 2005, her legacy of inspira-tion continues. For fifty years now, she has helped to change Baptist culture with her matter-of-fact attitude and her determination to be all that God called her to be despite the opposition she faced in seeking ordination and despite the challenges she encountered in finding a church in which to serve.

Addie's story began and ended in Covington, Virginia. She was born there on June 29, 1917, to a family of committed Baptists. Her paternal great-great-grandfather had been an itinerant Baptist preacher in Amherst County, near Lynchburg, Virginia.[1] He rode approximately three thousand miles a year on horseback, preaching the gospel every chance that he had.[2] Both Addie's maternal and paternal grandparents were faithful members of the Covington Baptist Church. In fact, four generation of Davises had wor-shiped in this church, and her maternal grandmother taught a Sunday school class there while her infant daughter, Addie's mother, sat in her lap.[3] Addie's parents were also active in this church and made sure that she and her two siblings "were always there when the church doors were open."[4] In addition to regular church attendance, the Davises stayed busy with their family busi-ness. Addie's father owned and ran a furniture store in Covington, and she spent much of her childhood at the store, helping her father.

Early in her life, Addie felt drawn to faith. In a 1985 interview, she recalled, "I was baptized between the ages of eight and nine. I have as long as I can remember had a very strong religious interest." Addie also began sensing a call to ministry but was uncertain as to what to do with this calling: "As a child, I felt a call to preach, but women were not preachers so I never expressed this openly."[5] But even though she did not talk openly about this calling, she tried on the preacher role. In her playtime, Addie often pre-tended to be a preacher, and even then, as a little girl, she knew she liked preaching.[6]

When Addie was eight years old, a teenage friend of hers died unex-pectedly. Her death affected Addie deeply, and she recalled,

> I think this acquaintance with death had a lot to do with my attitudes about life and the way I viewed it. No one in our family had died and didn't for quite some time, but she was so dear to us, and the fact that we knew, as children would say then, that she had gone to be with Jesus. Heaven always seemed closer to me, and I was never afraid of death because of this, and I think that the beauty of her life and her patience

and sweetness had its influence. . . . She was an exceptional person, well-loved by so many people . . . in her brief life.[7]

Throughout her childhood and teenage years, Addie continued to be active in church, and she diligently sought to understand the calling that God had placed in her heart. She faithfully attended the Girls' Auxiliary and Young Women's Auxiliary and for a time considered that God might be leading her toward the vocation of missions. "I have always had a very strong feeling for missions," she said. "In fact, I thought a lot about mission work, but I never felt I really had the stamina that it might take to go to some of the countries where I might like to have gone. But the religious intent was always in the back of my mind."[8]

The sense of calling to be a preacher that Addie continued to experience into her teenage years must have been confusing given that she had no role models for pastoral ministry. The lack of models and the limited options she saw before her as a teenage girl held her back from talking to family and friends about her calling to preach.

The other limitation that threatened Addie's calling was educational. Neither of her parents had received much formal education. Her father had to leave school at the age of fourteen to help support his family after his own father's death. He worked hard, saving as he could, and finally had enough money to open the furniture store in Covington. His lack of educational opportunity fostered in him the determination that all three of his children would go to college,[9] and finally, at the age of twenty-one, the time had come for Addie to go to college.

In 1938, Addie enrolled in Meredith College, a Baptist women's school in Raleigh, North Carolina. She majored in psychology and minored in speech, and upon graduation in 1942, she found a ministry position and began service as education director at the 500-member First Baptist Church in Elkin, North Carolina, a town just west of Winston-Salem and about three hours south of her hometown of Covington. Addie served the church for four years, and while this position allowed her to live into God's calling, she knew in her heart that she had not been called to be a religious educator but to be a pastor.[10] She left Elkin in 1946 to take the position of dean of women at Alderson-Broadus College, a Baptist school in Phillipi, West Virginia. In addition to her administrative duties at the school, Addie also occasionally taught psychology classes.

Serving and teaching at Alderson-Broadus led Addie to recognize her need for theological education and to strengthen her commitment to pursue her calling. She applied to and was accepted by both Duke Divinity School and Yale Divinity School, but as she prepared to make this transition, a need in her family took precedence. Her father had died in 1944, and following his death, Addie's mother took over management of the furniture store. By the end of the 1940s, her mother needed help with the store, and thus, instead of heading off to divinity school, Addie returned home to Covington. For over ten years, she worked alongside her mother, selling furniture. But Addie never gave up on her call to ministry.

During her decade at home, Lone Star Baptist Church, a rural congregation just sixteen miles outside of Covington, called Addie to serve as their interim pastor. She served in this position for six months. The interim role provided Addie with opportunities to preach and gave her invaluable pastoral experience.[11] The turning point for Addie during those years in Covington, however, was a health crisis. A bout with appendicitis and peritonitis became critical when the doctors failed to diagnosis her illness correctly. Addie's appendix burst during surgery, and her brush with death left her more determined to follow God's leadership.[12] During her recovery, Addie concluded, "If I was permitted to live, I will do what I've always felt in my heart I should do, which was to be a preacher."[13]

In 1960, Addie's mother retired, leaving her forty-three-year-old daughter free to pursue her dream of becoming a pastor. By this time, Southeastern Baptist Theological Seminary in Wake Forest, North Carolina, had begun allowing women to study for a Bachelor of Divinity degree, which is the equivalent to a current Master of Divinity degree, and Addie was among the first women to attend and graduate from the seminary. Her graduation program in 1963 lists the names of six women, including Addie's, among the 144 graduates that May.[14]

Despite the fact that she was greatly outnumbered by males in all her classes, Addie's decision to pursue her calling was not dampened. She soon realized, however, that she would need the support of the faculty and administration if she were going to be successful in finding ministry opportunities. Early in her days at Southeastern, she made an appointment with Syndor Stealey, the seminary's president, and shared with him about her calling and her desire to preach.

In her first semester of seminary, the fall semester of 1960, Addie took her first preaching class. She received favorable feedback from her professor and fellow students. The next summer, she took a class titled "Preaching to Human Need," in which she had to prepare six sermon outlines and one full-length sermon. The texts and titles for her sermon outline included

Luke 19:8—"Is Honesty Your Problem?"; James 1:19—"Coping with Anger"; Job 14:14—"Born to Die," and Psalm 46:1—"A Stormy Weather Faith." Although Addie had preached previously, she was still a novice at preparing and writing sermons in the seminary classroom setting, and she received "Bs" on her outlines. But she improved over the course of the brief summer semester, and on her full sermon, "Am I My Brother's Keeper?" (based on Genesis 4:9-16), Addie received an "A-minus," and her professor wrote comments such as "excellent outline," "worthy material," and "well handled." Addie included two notes to her professor at the end of this manuscript, which give some insight about her high expectations for herself and her awareness of her limitations: "Please note that I am not a professional typist. It is quite an ordeal for me to do a paper as neatly as I would like, and it is never without error; therefore, I hope you will take this into consideration as I cannot afford to have it done professionally." She also wrote, "This [sermon] came out somewhat longer than I expected. I normally give four pages in about twelve minutes, so this should run around twenty-five. In actually delivering it I would cut it to about twenty-two minutes which is usually my average length for a message."[15]

In that 1961 sermon, Addie courageously took on the greatest social justice issues of the day. She addressed racism, unethical business practices, and poverty, asking, "Will the color of skin continue to build a wall to divide us? Can we not build bridges of understanding? We do this as individuals occasionally. Most of us know Negros whom we regard highly and who are dear to us; but as a people, we have not bridged the gap of prejudice and misconception. This we need to begin to do, and we must start with ourselves." Addie also asked, "Should Christianity make any difference in our business practices? Are we ever guilty of false advertising, too much markup, overselling, or unreasonable interest rates?"

In the concluding paragraph of "Am I My Brother's Keeper?" Addie wrote,

> If we permit this transforming power of Christ to work in us we can expect that our attitudes will change and our actions will follow a different pattern. Through him that is at work in us it can be accomplished. When we determine that as far as we are concerned we will follow the leadership of his Spirit and be guided by his truth, then we will begin to live more and more like children of God. God is asking each one of us to be our brother's keeper. This is possible only as we live and act as children of the Most High![16]

Addie enrolled in a History of Christianity course in spring 1963, and for her class project she completed a paper titled "Illustrative Attitudes of the Contemporary Church toward the Ordination of Women." In her introduction, she wrote,

> Many people wonder why the question of the ordination of women should arise at all since, obviously, they themselves have not considered it, and see no particulate reason why it should be considered. It seems unbelievable to "traditional" thinkers that some denominations have admitted women to the ministry for a number of years, and do not feel that this is a man's prerogative alone.[17]

She then gave attention to the biblical interpretations most often cited by those opposing or defending women's roles in the church, provided information on the varied polity structures of denominations, and focused on the cultural influence on beliefs about ordination. In researching the paper, Addie read a wide cross-section of books on the subject, including Charles E. Raven, *Women and the Ministry*, 1929; John R. Rice, *Bobbed Hair, Bossy Wives and Women Preachers*, 1941; F. D. Bacon, *Women in the Church*, 1946; Cecilia M. Ady, *The Role of Women in the Church*, 1948; Kathleen Bliss, *The Service and Status of Women in the Churches*, 1952, Doris M. Rose, *Baptist Deaconesses*, 1954; Charles C. Ryrie, *The Place of Women in the Church*, 1958; and M. E. Thrall, *The Ordination of Women to the Priesthood*, 1958. While a good number of these resources offered negative views on the ordination of women ministers, Addie also found encouragement from some. In Thrall's book, she read, "In the matter of ordaining women we have not perhaps reached a clear enough understanding of the truth to make any decisive action necessary or possible. The vital question at the present moment is whether or not we are really and genuinely concerned to discover the truth."[18] Addie also quoted Raven in her paper: "If the Church is what it claims to be, the embodiment of the Spirit of Christ, then since His Spirit is manifestly operative through the ministry of women, that ministry must have its accredited place in the organism: otherwise the Church is not truly or completely the expression and instrument of the will of God."[19]

In her paper, Addie included statistical information regarding denominations associated with the World Council of Churches and their official stance with regard to women's ordination. She briefly reviewed the beliefs of Roman Catholics, Anglicans, Swedish Lutherans, Methodists, Presbyterians, Congregationalists, and both American and Southern Baptists. Her research of Southern Baptist annuals and records concluded with these words: "It is, therefore, evident that a local church could call for the ordination of women. According to the records available, no woman has yet been ordained in the Southern Baptist Convention."[20] Her research and her inclusion of this information in her seminary paper indicate that Addie clearly had awareness that should she seek ordination from a Southern Baptist church, she would be making history. Her research on women's ordination also indicates that she was educating herself, carefully and intentionally preparing herself for what was to come.

Addie devoted the final section of the paper to telling the stories of Margaret Blair Johnstone, a Congregational pastor, and Margaret K. Henrichsen, who also had served as a pastor. The concluding statement of the paper was a quote from Emil Brunner: "It is impossible to put down in black and white, as a universal rule, which spheres of activity 'belong' to a woman and which do not. This can only become clear through experience, and for this experience first of all the field must be thrown open."[21] Addie's professor gave her an "A-minus" on the paper and wrote "Very interesting."

During her seminary years, Addie was an active member of Watts Street Baptist Church in Durham. There she met Warren Carr, pastor of Watts Street. As she neared graduation, Addie knew that she needed to be licensed to preach. In early 1963, she talked with Carr about the possibility of the church's granting her a license. Both Carr and Watts Street "had achieved something of a reputation for their civil rights activism."[22] Most likely, the willingness of this church to take radical stands on racial issues made Addie comfortable in asking them to consider another radical stand—to endorse a woman preacher. Indeed, Carr and members of Watts Street, like many progressive Baptists in the 1960s, had begun to see that "it is illogical to take stands on behalf of black liberation and refuse to do so on behalf of the freedom of women to choose the ways to direct their service to the same God whose teachings mandated freedom for oppressed blacks."[23]

Looking back on the process of being licensed by Watts Street, Addie said,

> I felt that I had a friend in Warren Carr, and I approached him about whether or not he thought his church might back me in granting a license to preach with the idea of being ordained later. He said it sort of threw him at first, but being the kind of man he is, he said yes. And he laid the groundwork very patiently and quietly in the church among the people, and I am sure in the association among fellow pastors. As a result of that, I was granted a license to preach on March 13, 1963. This was just before

I graduated in May of that year. And we got snowed out two weeks before. That was a rough two weeks for me, waiting to see if I would be approved. And the church approved. It was a large business meeting, and they had been notified. . . . If anyone was opposed, then they must not have voted because I think the vote was unanimous as far as we can tell. There were well over one hundred people in attendance.[24]

In the minutes of that March 13, 1963, business meeting, the clerk recorded, "Recommended that Watts Street Church grant to Miss Addie E. Davis a license to preach. Miss Davis is a member of this church and will be graduated from Southeastern Baptist Theological Seminary in May, 1963."[25] The church presented Addie with her ministerial license that same evening following the vote. The Certificate of License she received was the standard fill-in-blank form sold by the Southern Baptist Convention's Broadman Press, and it read, "This is to certify Addie E. Davis who has given evidence that God has called him into THE GOSPEL MINISTRY was Licensed to preach the Gospel as he may have opportunity, and to exercise his gifts in the work of the Ministry by Watts Street Baptist Church at Durham, North Carolina on the thirteenth day of March, 1963." The certificate was signed by Eleanor S. Whitefield, the church clerk, and Warren Carr, pastor.[26] Obviously, Baptists, even progressive Baptists, had no concept

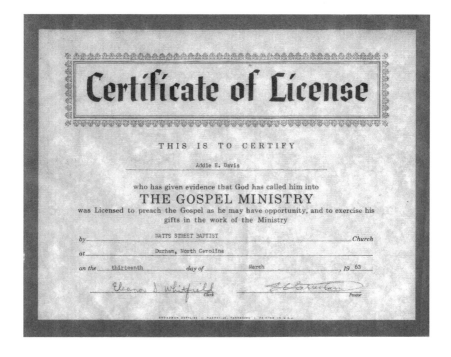

that a woman would even be licensed to preach, and they certainly had no certificates available that would have been appropriate to present to women ministers. Thus, Addie received her very masculine paperwork and was set free to use her gifts and to preach the gospel.

In addition to working toward licensure, Addie spent those months before graduation looking for a church to pastor. Wanting to stay in the South, she contacted several state executives about placement. None of the executives knew "of any church that would consider a woman," she recalled, "and the truth is that they weren't willing to recommend a woman to any church. I had the feeling that most of them were a little bit afraid to be the first to make a suggestion like this."[27]

Addie's search for a pastorate continued for over a year, and finally, after realizing that she would not find a Southern Baptist church open to her leadership, she contacted her college friend, Elizabeth Miller, who worked for the American Baptist Churches, USA. After college, Miller had been pastor of First Baptist Church in Readsboro, Vermont, and she knew that the church was without a minister. Miller recommended Addie for the position. Thus, in spring 1964, following a year-long search, Addie finally found a church that would talk to her. In June, Addie traveled to Vermont, interviewed with the search committee, and on Sunday, June 7, she preached to the congregation.

The church bulletin that day noted, "We are happy to WELCOME Miss Addie Davis to our pulpit today as our candidate and guest minister." Addie made notes on her bulletin as she prepared for worship, writing, "Oh come let us worship and bow down, let us kneel before the Lord, our maker. For he is our God, and we are people of his pasture and sheep of his land. Psa. 95:6-7." Apparently, she read these verses during the call to prayer. For another call to prayer later in the service, she wrote a note that said, "and it shall come to pass that before they call, I will answer; and while they are yet speaking, I will hear. Isa. 65:24." For the offertory words, she jotted down, "a poor, penniless Savior walking down the dusty road to Galilee said: 'It is more blessed to give than to receive.'" The bulletin also reminded members, "Today: Meeting of the Pulpit Committee directly after the close of the morning service."[28]

Following that meeting, the pulpit committee recommended forty-seven-year-old Addie Davis to be the church's pastor, and the congregation soon extended a call to her. With this invitation, Addie now needed to be ordained. She first approached her home church, Covington Baptist Church. She had grown up in that church, served there, and still had family connections in Covington. Addie was hopeful that the congregation would bless and affirm her new ministry.[29]

> The minister who was there at the time I went to the seminary was very much opposed to women ministers. I think the people in my church would have approved because I grew up there and they knew me. I had approached them about whether or not they would grant me a license to preach. . . . I had a letter from the chairman of the board of deacons at . . . Covington Baptist Church, stating that they were afraid it would create a controversy, which no doubt it would in most quarters. But I felt . . . that certainly the members would have approved, and my letter [asking for ordination] was addressed to the church, but of course, it apparently went to the minister and he took it to the board of deacons. So I simply withdrew the request. . . . And people still ask me why I was not ordained there, and I simply say, "Well, you had your chance." I did feel within me that I should give them the opportunity because there had been four generations of my family in that church. . . . But I simply felt that it was better to withdraw the request, which I did, because I did not want to be the center of any controversy.[30]

In a 2001 interview, Addie indicated that perhaps the opposition to her ordination came not from the pastor but from his wife, for after her death, the Covington pastor wrote Addie, affirming her decision to be ordained. Addie treasured this letter, saying that it provided great comfort to her over the years.[31]

After withdrawing her request from her home church, Addie contacted several churches in Raleigh about the possibility of their ordaining her. When those churches declined, she began to believe that she might never be ordained in a Southern Baptist church. Some of her friends told her that her quest was hopeless. Addie was aware that she could seek and be granted ordination by an American Baptist church, but as a lifelong Southern Baptist, she very much wanted to be affirmed by the denomination that had birthed and nurtured her faith and of which she had now been affiliated for forty-seven years.[32] She held on to that hope and contacted the church that had licensed her the year before. The deacons at Watts Street reviewed her request for ordination, and Warren Carr sat with Addie to talk about her calling. In a 1979 interview, he recounted his conversation with her, noting that she was certain that God had called her "to be a preacher." Not once, according to Carr, did Addie express a desire to be the first woman ordained by a Southern Baptist church, although she clearly was aware that she would most likely hold that honor of "being first."[33] He remembered her clearly stating her desire to fulfill the ministry to which God had called her. Thus, Addie's ordination "was solely due to her personal testimony," not an attempt to call attention to herself.[34]

During that conversation, Addie also told Carr, "I have tried to be almost everything having to do with ministry." Yet nothing could still her restlessness or enable her to let go of the knowledge that God had called her to be a pastor.[35] Her overwhelming sense of call overwhelmed Carr. He could not "escape the fact that she was called! She belonged in the center pulpit, according to our tradition, to proclaim the gospel on the Lord's Day. She was called to be a preacher."[36]

Carr proceeded to select an ordination council to examine Addie, and all council members promised to evaluate her based on her calling and confession. On the day of the examination, she was one of two candidates for ordination. The council voted to recommend the other candidate, the chaplain to Baptist students at Duke University, despite what they believed to be young man's unorthodox belief concerning the Virgin Birth. Addie's conservative theology posed no problems for the council, but two members confessed that despite their previous assurances, they could not recommend a woman for ordination. After a heated discussion, one supportive council member asked the two holdouts to explain their apprehension: "Brethren, you leave me confused. In the case of our first candidate, you were quite insistent that he believe that a Virgin bore the word. How is it that you are now so adamant that a virgin should not preach the word?"[37] The council ultimately voted unanimously to ordain Addie, with only one member abstaining.[38]

The ordination service at Watts Street Baptist Church was scheduled for 3:00 p.m. on August 9, 1964. Addie remembered the service as meaningful and noted that "the whole congregation wholeheartedly backed me."[39] John Davis, associate pastor at Watts Street, opened the service with a call to worship followed by the prayer of invocation. The congregation sang two hymns, "When I Survey the Wondrous Cross" and "O Jesus, I Have Promised." Laura Kendall, the guest soloist, sang "Love Never Faileth." Warren Carr preached the ordination sermon. Two of Addie's professors at Southeastern Seminary also participated. Luther Copeland, who taught Christian missions and world religions, offered the charge to the candidate. Copeland was then and would become even more so a strong advocate for Baptist women in ministry, and at his death in 2011, his obituary noted that "he was proud to have participated in the ordination of Addie Davis."[40]

The second professor, R. C. Briggs, who taught New Testament at Southeastern, led the ordination prayer. All the ordained ministers in attendance were invited to be part of the laying on of hands. The service concluded with the chairman of the Watts Street's board, V. A. Parks, Jr., presenting the newly ordained minister with a Bible, and Addie speaking the words of benediction.[41] While those in attendance and leading the service were aware of the specialness of the day, most likely they "remained largely unaware of the event's historic significance."[42]

Not everyone, of course, was supportive. Soon after the ordination, Carr received nearly fifty letters criticizing him and the church. Addie also was the target of criticism, which she had expected. Even so, the condemning letters surprised her, for in her thinking, "If I didn't agree with something, I certainly wouldn't sit down and write somebody I didn't even know my opinion on something that really wasn't any of my business, especially in the South where ordination is supposed to be within the realm of the local church."[43] But a handful of men did not hold Addie's views about staying out of the business of a local church, and they sent her scathing, hurtful letters. A Richmond, Virginia, man demanded, "Renounce your ordination!"[44] Another man told her to learn from her husband, an ironic demand given that Addie was unmarried.[45] Another labeled her "a child of the Devil."[46]

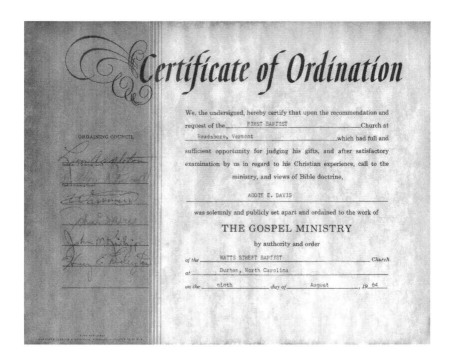

Addie "never bothered to answer any of them." Instead, she determined to "just take it as grain of salt and keep on."[47]

While Addie certainly encountered opposition, historian Elizabeth H. Flowers concluded that the ordination did not "create a storm of controversy across the Southern Baptist Convention."[48] For most Southern Baptists, the event went entirely unnoticed. Only one story about the ordination appeared in Baptist Press, the SBC's official news service, and in that article, the writer offered the comment that "women graduates of Southern Baptist seminaries usually enter church vocations in education or music, become teachers or are appointed as unordained missionaries."[49] At the next gathering of the Southern Baptist Convention in June 1965, Addie's name was not mentioned and the topic of women's ordination was not addressed—at least not from the floor.[50] Two years after the ordination, in 1966, Marie Mathis, president of the Woman's Missionary Union, was asked about women's ordination and replied, "I've never heard of a woman wanting to be a minister, and I've been connected with women's organizations in this faith since 1938. . . . I think it is women's intuitive feeling that ministers should be men."[51] Some scholars have asserted that Addie's ordination was an anomaly or aberration, which explains the lack of attention it received at the convention level.[52] They also have noted that Addie's move to the North to find ministry placement also lessened the impact of her ordination. Whether their analysis is correct or not, the fact is that for the next seven years, no other Southern Baptist woman was ordained. Another view is presented by Flowers, who eloquently concluded,

> One is hard-pressed to accept that the major milestone for Southern Baptist women in the twentieth century could be so easily forgotten. It seems more likely that Mathis and the WMU were intentionally avoiding any hint of controversy. Like their male counterparts, WMU officials operated from the center. If Davis's ordination became the symbol of progress for Southern Baptist women, as it was later touted, its downplaying also embodied the spirit of compromise that marked Southern Baptist life during the 1950s and early 1960s. By 1966, though, compromise was in jeopardy. The SBC was mired in an inerrancy debate, and despite the WMU's best efforts, women were soon to be implicated.[53]

But by 1966, Addie had relocated to Vermont and was happily serving her first church, First Baptist, Readsboro.

In August 1964, Addie moved from Virginia, settled into a new home, and was in the pulpit on Sunday, August 30. That day's church bulletin included a note about her arrival: "We are very happy to have Rev. Addie Davis with us today as our supply minister. Rev. Davis will assume the ministry of this church the first of September." The bulletin also offered an invitation: "Sunday, September 13 at 7:00 p.m. there will be an Installation Service and Reception for Rev. Addie E. Davis, who arrived Monday from Covington, Virginia, to be the minister of this church. Plan to attend this service and meet your Pastor."[54] The use of "Rev." along with Addie's name rather than "Miss," which was the title used for her during her previous visit in June, was the church's nod to her recent ordination, but no direct mention was made of that event. On that last Sunday in August, Addie preached a sermon titled "The Ministry of the Church," which is included in this collection.

Addie was the second woman to serve as the pastor of First Baptist, Readsboro, and in the earliest days of her tenure there, she discovered "little to no resistance to her" as a result of her gender. The attitude of her congregation was completely different from what she had encountered in the South.[55] One young girl in Addie's church could not fathom a man being a minister because she had only known women pastors. As the girl and her siblings were playing church, they took turns acting the part of ministers. When the girl's younger brother announced that he wanted to be the preacher, she responded incredulously, "You can't be the preacher; only women are preachers."[56] The male members quickly accepted Addie, and often called on her to handle what were then (and still often are) considered the more "masculine" tasks of meeting with contractors and making building maintenance decisions, because her background and experience made her more qualified in those areas than many of the male members.[57]

In 1964, the church at Readsboro had approximately 150 members. Because it was the only Protestant church in town, the congregation included many non-Baptist members. Thus, these early days of her ministry shaped Addie's interest in and passion for ecumenism.

Like all pastors, Addie spent much time planning worship, attending and leading meetings, and visiting members in the hospital. The September 13, 1964, church bulletin noted two meetings to be held that week: the pastor's cabinet was to meet on September 15 and Sunday church school teachers were to meet on September 17. That week's bulletin also reminded members to "Remember in Prayer and with a card" several hospitalized members.[58] While at First Baptist, Addie gave much of her time to pastoral care, or what she called "in-depth ministry." As a single person, she felt that she could invest herself in ways that married ministers could not:

I spent a great deal of time with people, and of course, I could stay much longer because I didn't have a family waiting for me at home. I realized that this wouldn't be feasible for everyone. But this is one of my strengths—compassion. I have had so many people say to me, "You were there when we needed you." So I spent many long hours in hospitals with people who were having surgery, recovering from illness, and for the most part, whenever I could, I went every day, no matter how far the distance was.[59]

She sought to model her ministry on Jesus' compassion-based style of service. Christ "had all the gentleness and the compassion and the sympathy, yet he was very strong and courageous and had all the qualities that we can think of that would be worthwhile."[60]

On her first anniversary at First Baptist, September 5, 1965, Addie offered these words to her congregation:

> Since this is the beginning of our second year together, it is fitting for me to express again my gratitude for your many kindnesses to me in so many ways. My family and friends in Virginia send their greetings and appreciation to you also. It is my hope that in the coming year we may experience a greater depth of love and a stronger bond of unity such as should always characterize those who dwell in Christ and belong to His Church. It is only by His power at work within us that we can accomplish any good and bear fruit in His Kingdom. Toward this goal I would call upon you to join with me as together we commit ourselves anew to Jesus Christ and the mission of the Church which is our mutual responsibility.[61]

During her years in Vermont, Addie was active in her community and among Baptists in the state. She participated in the Windham Baptist Association, serving on several committees. She was active in the Vermont Baptist State Convention and was elected recorder in 1969. In 1971, the Vermont State Baptist Convention named her Vermont's pastor of the year, an impressive accomplishment for someone who had just seven years earlier wondered if she would ever pastor a church.[62] On June 25, 1972, Addie submitted her resignation, having accepted the pastorate of Second Baptist Church of East Providence, Rhode Island. She had served the Readsboro church for eight years, and in her parting words to her parishioners, she wrote, "For the kind and thoughtful things which you have done for me I wish to express my deep appreciation . . . . To those of you who have remained faithful in your commitment to the Lord and His Church, I am doubly grateful."[63]

Leaving Vermont must have been difficult, but Addie felt a strong call to her new church in Rhode Island. She began her pastorate there on September 17, 1972, and an installation service (whose program can be found in the Appendix) held on September 24 was attended by James M. Webb of the Rhode Island State Council of Churches, W. Eugene Motter of the Rhode Island Baptist State Convention, and Glenn H. Payne of the East Providence Ministers' Association, all of whom brought greetings on behalf of their organizational bodies. During the service, the congregation pledged Addie their support:

> We, the members of the Second Baptist Church do hereby install the Rev. Addie E. Davis as minister this church. We solemnly pledge to walk with her in unity of spirit, in the bond of peace, and in all the ways of God known to us or to be made known unto us. We furthermore pledge such faithfulness in worship and work, and such loyalty to Christ and His Church in stewardship of our talents and possessions, as will advance the Kingdom of God in our church and in our community.[64]

Serving in "Roger Williams' territory," Addie continued to be a pioneer. She was the first woman pastor of this church. She was also Rhode Island's first woman pastor, the first woman elected to the Providence Baptist Theological Circle, and the first woman vice president of the East Providence Clergy Association.[65] Addie later served as president of the association, which consisted mostly of Catholic priests. Once again, Addie found herself immersed in ecumenical work, which proved to be a lifelong passion and commitment.[66]

During her ministry at the East Providence, which had a membership of approximately 250, the area was predominately Catholic, and in the 1970s, many Portuguese Catholics moved into the area.[67] Addie's church sponsored a Portuguese Baptist mission.

> We sponsored a family who came over from Portugal. This was a Baptist minister who wanted to come to this country but couldn't without someone to sponsor him. But they couldn't get that project going too well. They canvassed house to house and had a small group, but it never really took fire like it should have [because] there was a strong Portuguese [Baptist] church in Providence.[68]

The coming of the Portuguese not only presented Addie's church with mission opportunities; it also presented them with a dilemma.

A lot of the younger families had moved out to other areas, where they have built other churches. In fact, our church was offered some land to rebuild in one of the growing areas in East Providence but turned it down because . . . some older people get attached to the building. It is a beautiful church, a beautiful sanctuary. And they just felt that they could not give up their church. . . . Some of them . . . were older and they were not able to build another church, but I am sure they could have. And later, they felt they should have made that move, perhaps in earlier years. But it is still a very active church and has a real witness.[69]

Addie found that her gender did not impede her ministry at East Providence. Although the congregation had taken a bit of time in adjusting before they accepted her leadership, she discovered her new church to be warm and welcoming of her.[70] After many years of ministering in New England, Addie concluded that, once they found a minister to be worthy and to have integrity, the people there wholeheartedly supported the ministry of that person.[71]

During these years in which Addie pastored in New England, the women's movement in the United States was gaining momentum, and women's rights became a hotly debated issue. The same year in which Addie was licensed to preach, Betty Friedan's influential book, *The Feminist Mystique*, was released and soon became a best-seller. Friedan shocked Americans with her honest assessment of many women's dissatisfaction as a result of imposed gender roles. That same year, Congress passed the Equal Pay Act, making it illegal for employers to pay women less than men solely based on gender. The next year, the year in which Addie was ordained and began her pastorate in Vermont, the Civil Rights Act with the addition of Title VII banned discrimination based on race and gender, and the Equal Employment Opportunity Commission was created to investigate violations of the new laws. Two years later, in 1966, a new advocacy group, the National Organization for Women (NOW), was founded, and in 1971, the year that Addie accepted her second pastorate in Rhode Island, *Ms. Magazine* published its first "sample" issue. Gloria Steinem, its editor, soon stepped forward as a vocal advocate for the women's movement. The following year, Congress passed the Equal Rights Amendment (ERA) and sent it to the states to be ratified. Ten years later the amendment died, failing to receive enough support from the states. Some Southern Baptist leaders were among the vocal supporters of the ERA, including Jimmy Allen, who was president of the Southern Baptist Convention in 1979. But Southern Baptists soon turned in a different direction, and proponents of women's rights became hard to find among convention leadership.[72]

While Addie never spoke out publicly about the ERA, she was very much aware of the increasing importance of the women's movement, and she saw the connections between what was happening in American society and the gospel that she was preaching every Sunday. Among her papers, Addie had numerous pamphlets and mimeographed copies of articles that addressed the topic, including a pamphlet titled "Feminism and the Church Today" and a long article written by Leonard Swidler in 1971 titled "Jesus Was a Feminist." Swidler, professor of Catholic thought and interreligious dialogue at Temple University in Philadelphia, wrote the article for *Catholic World*, and in his concluding paragraph, he said, "From this evidence it should be clear that Jesus vigorously promoted the dignity and equality of women in the midst of a very male-dominated society: Jesus was a feminist, and a very radical one. Can his followers attempt to be anything less—*De Imitatione Christi.*"[73]

Addie apparently used these materials to prepare for a retreat she led during her time as pastor of East Providence. Although her typed notes are undated and her name is not listed as the writer, the handwriting on the notes and the instructions to herself indicate that these were most likely materials she produced. The retreat was titled "In God's Image: Male and Female," and the first discussion time was to given to the questions, "What does feminism mean to me? What was your first encounter with feminism?"[74] The plenary session of the retreat was devoted to the biblical implications of feminism, and the descriptive statement of that session noted, "The Gospel speaks of liberation of those oppressed, but there are other passages which are oppressive to women. What do we do with this dilemma?"[75] Addie was certainly echoing the hard questions being asked in the 1970s in society, but she was also asking those questions in the context of the church. Addie also kept a mimeographed copy of a Bible study agenda. It is not clear whether she wrote and taught this study or simply attended it. Titled "Bible Study on Women," the session outline called for a review of ten Scripture passages, including several of the more challenging ones: 1 Corinthians 11:1-16 and 1 Timothy 2:8-15. The outline also included questions about each passage that encouraged the participants to discuss the historical context of the Scriptures and to address Jesus' view of women in his own society.

Addie also kept in her possession two pamphlets. One titled "My Pastor's a Woman," produced by the American Baptist Churches, was based on findings from a task force on women in ministry convened by ABC of Massachusetts. The second pamphlet, titled "Feminism and the Church Today," was published by the National Ministries of the American Baptist Church, USA, under the direction of project manager, L. Faye Ignatius. The pamphlet called American Baptists to "work for full and equal use of women's resources in every area of church life, including pastoral ministry," and to "develop ways of giving support to persons dealing with the changing roles of women and men in church and society."[76]

Times were surely changing, and some Baptists were at least talking about inclusion of women in pastoral leadership roles. By the early 1980s, Southern Baptists had officially begun a decade-long stormy controversy that included heated conflict over the roles of women in the church. As that controversy officially got underway, sixty-five-year-old Addie left New England. In 1982, after ten years at East Providence, she resigned her position at Second Baptist Church. She left Rhode Island and returned to Covington, Virginia. Addie did not view this as a retirement from ministry, but instead a return home.

> I came back . . . mostly because of my family situation. Mother died, and she wanted me to keep our home, and my brother had died before she did. I only have a sister and some in-laws and one niece and nephew left. . . . We had always been a close family. So I either had to decide to sell the home or to take care of it. . . . Mother . . . always wanted me to have a place to come to, and I am very appreciative of that. There is no place like home. And naturally, I had no property or accumulation to amount to anything being in the ministry.[77]

Upon her return to the South, with seventeen years of pastoral experience, Addie hoped to find a Baptist church near Covington to pastor. She was surprised by an even more conservative attitude toward women in ministry among Southern Baptists: "I had expected to be able to pick up my work and take up another church. . . . But I am surprised by the ultra-conservative attitude which I have found since returning."[78] Not finding a Baptist church to pastor, however, did not end Addie's ministry. In 1983, she was invited to serve at Rich Patch Union Church, a rural ecumenical church in Alleghany County.

Rich Patch, founded in 1893, was a gathering of members from four different denominational backgrounds. Addie described the congregation as "ecumenical before the rest of us knew the meaning of the word."[79] When she joined the church, she became the sole ordained clergy person, and thus she was the one to whom members turned to perform weddings, baptisms, and funerals. She also spent a good amount of time visiting the sick and the elderly in the community. Addie loved the small, rural, ecumenical church because, as she told an interviewer in 1985, "It gives me an opportunity to serve and keeps me from getting stale."[80] Addie also served as pulpit supply for churches in the area and often attended her home church, First Baptist of Covington, where she was much loved and respected, although her calling and ministry were still not understood or accepted by all.[81]

During her long ministry, Addie became an inspirational hero for many Baptist women to whom she repeatedly gave the same advice: persevere. "Don't give up," she encouraged women, "if you have a call from God to enter the ministry."[82] In a June 1985 sermon at a Baptist Women in Ministry meeting in Dallas, Texas, Addie offered a few more words of advice and reflections on her years of ministry.

> One. You cannot afford to be bitter. I have seen those who are in both the North and South. We may suffer indignities and vocal opposition, but bitterness has a way of turning inward and hurting the one who harbors it. It diminishes our witness and hurts our cause. . . .
>
> Two. Set your priorities, your aims and goals with proper assessment of your abilities and determine to be the best of whatever you are—to give credence to your calling by adequate preparation, prayer, study and continuing education. The most important factor is to know the Lord so that no one can doubt your sincerity. Sincerity alone is not enough. Our foes are sincere, but, as we believe, sincerely wrong in their interpretation of scripture and their opposition to women pastors and deacons. Baptists have always stood for soul competency and allowed for diversity of opinion while cooperating to carry out the Great Commission.
>
> Three. We are called to preach the gospel. I have long been aware of the importance of preaching, having had some excellent preachers in my life. There is a scarcity of great preaching today because we have come to emphasize so many other things which are important but should not take away from the art of preaching. . . .
>
> We need to study the word—let God speak to us;
> To preach the Word—be well prepared;
> To live the Word—example is important;
> To be the word—the authentic messenger of God to others.
>
> Four. We need to encourage one another and be careful "not to kill the dreams of others." We are in this together and need all the encouragement we can give to each other. . . . You and I have had and have our

dreams. We may have experienced some suffering and pain in realizing them. Don't let the dream die; don't settle for less than you feel called of God to accomplish. Encourage one another, and especially those who are younger. It is worth what it takes to make this pilgrimage of faith in largely unchartered waters. In many ways, mine has been a lonely journey, but it is most rewarding and fulfilling. My dream came true!

Finally, I believe we authenticate our ministry by being who we are, the person God intended us to be. We are not carbon copies—each one is unique, redeemed and called of God to fulfill a particular ministry. BE YOURSELF! . . . Your gift to God and the people you serve is YOU— you're one of a kind.[83]

Addie closed this sermon with a benediction:

May God richly bless each of you as you follow your dream; and, hopefully, as God opens doors so long shut by prejudice and lack of understanding, He will continue to unfold His will for modern day women. The frontier is limitless in the realm of God's spirit. We humans become the stumbling blocks, often holding back the free flow of God's spirit. Women have always been pioneers, so keep on dreaming and cherish the dream God has given you! YOU WILL BE DELIVERED FROM EXILE!![84]

On August 8, 2004, Watts Street celebrated the fortieth anniversary of Addie's ordination to the ministry. Addie attended the worship service and preached a brief sermon titled "Four Important Words."

When we accepted the Lord Jesus, were baptized and joined the church, we made a *Commitment* to follow Jesus, to honor God with our lives, to keep His commandments and to serve him to the best of our ability.

He is the source of all our blessings, the one who created us and wants us to do His will, and to rely upon Him for life and all our needs.

Commitment is walking in fellowship with God, keeping our minds and hearts open to His spirit and His indwelling presence. When we fail to do this, He is there to help us try again. Each day offers a new beginning, and God loves us despite our failures. . . .

Secondly, we are called upon to place our *Trust* in Him, knowing that whatever we need He will supply according to what is best for us. In all of life's ups and downs, God is there to share our lives and to help us, to lift us and to enable us to keep on keeping on. . . . Faith grows as we trust God and walk faithfully with Him. Our trust increases, and we become mature Christians, able to digest solid food, spiritual food which deepens our faith as we come to trust Him more fully. . . .

The third word is *Rest*. Many people face life tired all the time because of insufficient rest. We were created to need rest. Sleep renews our bodies and gives us the physical strength we need each day. . . .

Remember the words of the hymn:

Drop thy still dews of quietness,
Till all our strivings cease;
Take from our souls the strain and stress,
And let our ordered lives confess
The beauty of thy peace.[85]

The fourth word is *Wait*. We find it hard to wait; we want instant satisfaction, instant answers to prayer. If we are sick, we want to get well fast. We want our problems solved quickly. Waiting is not one of our best characteristics.

We are told by the psalmist to "wait on the Lord; be of good courage and he will strengthen your heart." Psalm 27:14

Isaiah reminds us "those who wait on the Lord shall renew their strength, they shall mount up with wings like eagles, they shall run and not be weary, they shall walk and not faint." Isaiah 40:31

We wait to receive God's blessings. His timing is perfect although we may not understand why we have to wait. We know He is with us. He tells us to pray and to wait.[86]

At the time of this anniversary celebration, Addie was eighty-seven years old and was living in Covington, serving as a caregiver for her nephew, Luther Davis.[87] She was still serving the Rich Patch Union Church, preaching once a month, leading a monthly women's Bible study, and doing "right much hospital visiting."[88]

Just over a year later, on December 3, 2005, Addie passed away. Her death came after a brief illness. Her funeral was held four days later in Covington.[89] News of her death reminded moderate and progressive Baptists of the gift Addie Davis had been. In the days just after her funeral, when I was asked for a comment about her contributions, I responded,

She served, and will continue to serve, as a role model to the many Baptist women who have followed in her footsteps. What made Addie Davis so remarkable was not her place in history as the first woman to be ordained by a Southern Baptist church; it was her humility, her compassion, and her warm spirit. She faithfully followed God's calling, serving three churches as pastor or co-pastor. Her focus in those churches was on caring for the people and being with them in times of crisis.[90]

Indeed, Addie was a remarkable human being, a persistent and compassionate woman, a gifted pastor, and a woman of great humility. Baptists could not have selected a better person to be "first."

Of all Addie's many admirable qualities, perhaps the greatest was her faithfulness. She clung faithfully to the dream that God placed in her heart, even though dreams such as hers are often dangerous and involve risk. In her 1985 sermon at the Baptist Women in Ministry meeting, she proclaimed that "a dream born of God within one's heart should be heeded. Human forces may try to defeat us, but the strong of heart will keep trying, not willing to have that dream destroyed."[91] Addie encouraged women to "keep on dreaming and cherish the dream God has given you!"[92] In an interview the next day, she echoed that theme: "My advice is always, if you have a dream, follow it. . . . Mine came true. It can be done."[93]

Notes

1. Portions of this chapter originally appeared in Keith E. Durso and Pamela R. Durso, "'Cherish the Dream God Has Given You': The Story of Addie Davis," in *Courage and Hope: The Stories of Ten Baptist Women Ministers* (Macon GA: Mercer University Press, 2005) 18–30.

2. Addie Davis, interview by Eljee Bentley, 9 June 1985, tape recording, Alma Hunt Library of the Woman's Missionary Union, Birmingham AL.

3. Ibid.

4. Cody Lowe, "Pioneer: First Female Southern Baptist Pastor Says She Has No Regrets," *The Roanoke Times*, 28 August 2004, http://ww2.roanoke.com/extra/9887.html (accessed 20 January 2014).

5. Davis, interview by Bentley.

6. Lowe, "Pioneer."

7. Davis, interview by Bentley.

8. Ibid.

9. Lowe, "Pioneer."

10. Addie Davis, interview by Robin McKenzie (Hardison), 25 October 2001, in Addie Davis Papers, Special Collections, Jack Tarver Library, Mercer University, Macon GA.

11. Ibid. Addie did not remember the exact dates of her interim pastorate, only that it was sometime during the 1950s.

12. Addie Davis, interview by Pamela R. Durso, 8 December 2004.

13. Davis, interview by Bentley.

14. Addie Davis, graduation program, Southeastern Baptist Theological Seminary, Wake Forest NC, May 1963, in Addie Davis Papers, Special Collections, Jack Tarver Library, Mercer University, Macon GA. The six women graduates were Margaret Bloom, Addie Davis, Dorothy Deering, Laura Kendall, Judy McLamb, and Ida Marie Parker.

15. Addie Davis, "Miscellaneous papers and study guide," Addie Davis Papers, Jack Tarver Library.

16. Ibid.

17. Addie Davis, "Paper: 'Illustrative Attitudes of the Contemporary Church toward the Ordination of Women, 1963," Addie Davis Papers, Jack Tarver Library.

18. M. E. Thrall, *The Ordination of Women to the Priesthood* (London: SCM Press, LTD, 1958) 112, quoted in Davis, "Illustrative Attitudes."

19. Charles E. Raven, *Women in the Ministry* (New York: Doubleday, Doran and Company, 1929) 88, quoted in Davis, "Illustrative Attitudes."

20. Davis, "Illustrative Attitudes."

21. Emil Brunner, *Divine Imperative*, trans. Olive Wyon (Philadelphia: Westminster Press, 1947) 376, quoted in Davis, "Illustrative Attitudes."

22. Elizabeth H. Flowers, *Into the Pulpit: Southern Baptist Women and Power Since World War II* (Chapel Hill: University of North Carolina Press, 2012) 28.

23. David Stricklin, *A Genealogy of Dissent: Southern Baptist Protest in the Twentieth Century* (Lexington: University of Kentucky Press, 1990) 120.

24. Davis, interview by Bentley.

25. Church minutes, Watts Street Baptist Church, Durham NC, 13 March 1963, Addie Davis Papers, Jack Tarver Library, Mercer University, Macon GA.

26. Addie Davis, "Certificate of License," Addie Davis Papers, Jack Tarver Library, Mercer University, Macon GA.

27. Davis, interview by Bentley.

28. Church bulletin, First Baptist Church, Readsboro VT, 7 June 1964, Addie Davis Papers, Jack Tarver Library, Mercer University, Macon GA.

29. Davis, interview by McKenzie.

30. Davis, interview by Bentley.

31. Davis, interview by McKenzie.

32. Ibid.

33. "What Ever Happened to Addie Davis?" *Called and Committed*, February 1979, 1.

34. George Sheridan, "Tremors of Change," *Home Missions*, May 1972, 26.

35. "Reflections on the August 9, 1964 Ordination of Addie Davis: Written upon the Celebration of the Fortieth Anniversary of this Ordination August 8, 2004," church bulletin, Watts Street Baptist Church, Durham NC, 8 August 2004.

36. Ibid.

37. Ibid. See also Sheridan, "Tremors of Change," 27, and "What Ever Happened to Addie Davis?" 1.

38. Davis, interview by Bentley.

39. "What Ever Happened to Addie Davis?" 1; Lowe, "Pioneer."

40. "Edwin Luther Copeland: Obituary, November 19, 2011," http://brightfunerals.com/obituaries.php?page=0&op=view&id=1234.

41. Church bulletin, Watts Street Baptist Church, Durham NC, 9 August 1964, Addie Davis Papers, Jack Tarver Library.

42. Flowers, *Into the Pulpit*, 28.

43. "What Ever Happened to Addie Davis?" 1.

44. Lowe, "Pioneer."

45. Laura Johnson and John Pierce, "'A Day to Remember': N.C. Church Marks 40th Anniversary of First Female Southern Baptist Minister's Ordination," *Baptists Today*, October 2004, 38.

46. Addie Davis, "A Dream to Cherish," *Folio*, Autumn 1985, 1.

47. Davis, interview by Bentley.

48. Flowers, *Into the Pulpit*, 28.

49. "Church Ordains Woman to Pastoral Ministry," *Baptist Press*, 12 August 1964.

50. Flowers, *Into the Pulpit*, 28.

51. "Southern Baptists Tell Why 'Ministry Is for Men Only,'" *Detroit News*, 24 May 1966, quoted in Flowers, *Into the Pulpit*, 28.

52. David T. Morgan, *Southern Baptist Sisters: In Search of Status, 1845–2000* (Macon GA: Mercer University Press, 2003) 174.

53. Flowers, *Into the Pulpit*.

54. Church bulletin, First Baptist Church, Readsboro VT, 30 August 1964, Addie Davis Papers, Jack Tarver Library.

55. Davis, interview by McKenzie.

56. Davis, interview by Bentley; Davis, "A Dream to Cherish," 1; "What Ever Happened to Addie Davis?" 4.

57. Davis, interview by McKenzie.

58. Church bulletin, First Baptist Church, Readsboro VT, 13 September 1964, Addie Davis Papers, Jack Tarver Library.

59. Davis, interview by Bentley.

60. Ibid.

61. Church bulletin, First Baptist Church, Readsboro VT, 5 September 1965, Addie Davis Papers, Jack Tarver Library.

62. "What Ever Happened to Addie Davis?" 1; Davis, interview by McKenzie.

63. "Sermons and Bulletins, 1972," 2 July 1972, Addie Davis Papers, Jack Tarver Library.

64. Order of service, Second Baptist Church, East Providence RI, 24 September 1972, Addie Davis Papers, Jack Tarver Library.

65. "What Ever Happened to Addie Davis?" 4.

66. Davis, interview by McKenzie.

67. Davis, interview by Bentley; Lowe, "Pioneer."

68. Davis, interview by Bentley.

69. Ibid.

70. Davis, interview by McKenzie.

71. Ibid.

72. For an excellent and comprehensive analysis of Southern Baptists and their response to the women's movement, see Elizabeth Flowers's *Into the Pulpit: Southern Baptist Women and Power Since World War II*.

73. "Feminism and the Church Today," and Leonard Swidler, "Jesus Was a Feminist," Addie Davis Papers, Tarver Library, Mercer University, Macon GA. A transcript of Swidler's 1971 article may be found at http://godswordtowomen.org/feminist.htm (accessed 22 January 2014).

74. "Bible Study on Women" and "In God's Image: Male and Female," Addie Davis Papers, Jack Tarver Library, Mercer University, Macon GA.

75. Ibid.

76. "My Pastor's a Woman" and "Feminism and the Church Today," Addie Davis Papers, Jack Tarver Library Mercer University, Macon GA.

77. Davis, interview by Bentley.

78. Ibid.

79. Davis, "A Dream to Cherish," 8.

80. Davis, interview by Bentley.

81. Davis, interview by McKenzie.

82. "What Ever Happened to Addie Davis?" 4.

83. Davis, "A Dream to Cherish," 8.

84. Ibid.

85. From the hymn, "Dear Lord and Father of Mankind."

86. Addie Davis, "Four Important Words," sermon, Watts Street Baptist Church, Durham NC, 8 August 2004, 2. See also Cody Lowe, "Pioneer Preacher Abides in Patience and Realism," *Roanoke Times*, 29 August 2004.

87. Luther and his sister, Beth, a medical doctor in Oregon, were Addie's only remaining relatives.

88. Davis, interview by Bentley.

89. "Addie Davis, First Woman Ordained as Southern Baptist Pastor, Dies at 88," Associated Baptist Press, 9 December 2005.

90. Ibid.

91. Davis, "A Dream to Cherish," 1.

92. Ibid.

93. Davis, interview by Bentley.

Chapter One

Waiting for You
(Isaiah 6:1-8)

Addie Davis

When Harvard University celebrated her 300th anniversary, some freshmen held up a placard which read, "This institution has waited 300 years for us!" In a sense, the sign holders were right. And today, that is my message for you: the Woman's Missionary Union has waited for you to celebrate its centennial, and you young people and graduates have waited what seems like a long time to you to receive these awards, your high school or college diplomas. We have waited for you!

Your achievements represent hard work and dedication—a milestone— but you will discover that there are no resting places, just breathers along the way, for you must get on with the tasks of missions, education, and employment. You must certainly get on with the business of living.

You who are young still have decisions to make concerning your life's work. You must discern what is it you feel called to do. You must discover how you can best use your God-given talents to make an investment of your life, while at the same time deriving real joy in living, serving, and being who you are supposed to be.

Isaiah answered the call of God as he encountered God's holiness while worshiping in the temple. Feeling cleansed and purified from sin, Isaiah responded, "Here am I, send me!" We have lost something of our sense of the holiness of God and our own unworthiness in light of God's goodness. God is always "other than," "more than," and beyond all that we can fully comprehend. God chose to be revealed to us not only in the prophets and others who have gone before, but God chose to be revealed primarily through the life of Jesus. We need only examine Jesus' life and teachings to see how far short we fall in being the persons God intended.

As we enter into partnership with God in faith, whether now in the beginning of the second century of WMU or in the beginning of whatever it is that God is calling us to do both as young people and older, we can be sure that God does not call us to do something that we are incapable of doing. God calls us to use the natural and developed gifts that are ours. No matter how small or how great our talents, our gifts are multiplied and strengthened in the hands of God.

Remember Jesus' parable about the master who gave talents to his servants. We find that parable in Matthew 25, and we read of the master who condemned the one-talent servant because he failed to use or to invest what he had been given. That one talent seemed so small and unimportant.

You who are young have a lifetime to invest, and the questions for you are: Will you invest your life in the kingdom of God? Will you be sure to develop those personal qualities that cause you to invest wisely rather than selfishly? Will you be concerned with what you can give rather than what you can get? Remember that you are unique; God has made no two of us alike. And remember this is your day. Now is your turn. The world waits to see what you will do, and God waits expectantly for you.

Remember that other folks have made an investment in your life—all the missionaries who have ever lived and those who now serve throughout our world; your pastors and Sunday school teachers; your parents and grand-parents; and those who struggled for religious liberty, especially our Baptist heroes such as Roger Williams and those earliest Baptists here in our country who founded a small church in Providence, Rhode Island. This weekend, on June 5, 1988, that church, the First Baptist Church in America, is celebrating 350 years of freedom and Baptist beginnings in North America. Incidentally, this historic church to which we all trace our roots now has a woman pastor—and religious freedom has struck a new note.[1] Remember that there are so many who gave so much to make it possible for you and for all of us to experience soul freedom, that we might have the opportunity to grapple for ourselves and to interpret the Bible according to the leadership of the Holy Spirit, and that we might live a life of order that we understand to be Lord-given and Lord-inspired.

We take so much for granted as Americans. We forget our obligation to those who have gone before us, and as one has reminded us, "We need to pay rent on the space we occupy." To me, I believe we need to render back to God a "thank you" for all that God has invested in us through prophets, such as Isaiah, through the peoples of old, through the life and ministry of Jesus, through Jesus' disciples, through those early Christians, and through all who have contributed to our religious heritage over the centuries. We dare not take their sacrifices for granted. They paid a high cost.

Today, remember that God called you, and as young people and older adults, you are called to search out and listen to what God is saying in this generation. God is not confined to the past. God is the God of the present and the future as well. And there is much work God still needs us to do. Not everything has been done that needs to be accomplished in order to right the wrongs in our churches and in ourselves.

The world has waited all these years for you. Surely, the needs and challenges have never been greater in our world. The world needs us to share our faith and to live in light of God's revealed truth. Paul, in 2 Corinthians 5:19, reminds us that God is in Christ reconciling the world, and God is calling us to be ambassadors of reconciliation. That is, God is making an appeal through us. God chose to use human beings to accomplish his purposes, which means we need a word from God within us. We can respond to all the brokenness we see in our world, all the fractured relationships for which we do not have all the answers. And we are assured that we have a loving, forgiving, compassionate God who walks with us. We have Jesus who became flesh and dwelt among us and who called to us, saying, "I am the way. Follow me." Jesus gives us a sense of direction. Jesus also gives us intelligence and the will to follow.

If we are to find wholeness or healing, where else can we go except to God, who created us, and to Jesus, who died for us and who waits to redeem all facets of our lives? We must remember that we become fully human only when touched by the divine. In other words, we are God's children, given to live in this particular time as the people of God, called to invest our lives for the present and future generations.

As Harry Emerson Fosdick wrote in the hymn, "God of Grace and God of Glory," "Grant us wisdom, grant us courage for the living of these days."[2] To live for self and self alone is to miss the meaning of life. To live for God and to express this in relation to others, as Jesus lived, is to find a fuller life here on earth with deeper spiritual meaning, and to have eternal life someday with God.

The challenge has never been greater—the lost, the confused, the homeless, and the desperate are out there waiting to know that God cares and to know that God loves them. The challenges for young people also have never been greater. You have so many opportunities and fields of service open to you—all of which call for your best! If you dedicate yourself to following God and allow yourself to be guided by the Spirit, you will be amazed at what you can do. What takes place in the church, what is done for missions, what is accomplished in our world, I believe, is up to us. The choices we make help determine the outcome. God is waiting for us.

Frederick Potter Woods reminds us of these truths in his poem, "Talents":

> Stir up the gifts of God which are in thee
> Wrote Paul to Timothy;
> And as a steward of His gifts I know
> God asks the same of me.
>
> What can I do? My talent seems so small
> It's hardly worth the deed;
> But when I use the best I have for God
> It grows to meet the need.
>
> A world to build anew, ideals lift up;
> And all in fields of white,
> Till now I see the harvest lives with me,
> Lord, help me build myself.[3]

The future is on your doorstep. God is waiting for you!

"Waiting for You" was preached at Covington Baptist Church, Covington, Virginia, on Sunday, June 5, 1988. On that Sunday, the church was celebrating the 100th anniversary of the Woman's Missionary Union (1888–1988) and recognizing recent high school graduates.

Notes

1. Kate Harvey Penfield was pastor of First Baptist Church, Providence, Rhode Island, from 1987 to 1995.

2. Harry Emerson Fosdick, "God of Grace, and God of Glory."

3. Frederick Potter Woods, "Talents," unknown source.

Chapter Two

The Ministry of the Church
(Ephesians 4:1-16)

Addie Davis

The church has certain primary functions or ministries that we ought to keep uppermost in our minds. It is about these that we are thinking today. First of all, let me say that I conceive of the church as being under the Lordship of Jesus Christ, and that we have the promised leadership of the Holy Spirit in the ministry of the church. In John 15 and 16, Jesus says,

> But when the Counselor comes, whom I shall send to you from the Father, even the Spirit of truth, who proceeds from the Father, he will bear witness to me; and you also are witnesses, because you have been with me from the beginning. (John 15:26-27)

> I have yet many things to say to you, but you cannot bear them now. When the Spirit of truth comes, he will guide you into all the truth; for he will not speak his own authority, but whatever he hears he will speak, and he will declare to you the things that are to come. He will glorify me, for he will take what is mine and declare it to you. All that the Father has is mine; therefore I said that he will take what is mine and declare it to you. (John 16:12-15)

Thus, the New Testament concept of the church is that it is directed by the Spirit of God.

Actually, the church is the continuing ministry of Jesus Christ in the world, and so conceived places upon us a tremendous responsibility. We are witnesses for him and to the truth that he wants declared to the world. The church is made up of redeemed sinners who have partaken of the grace of God. In response to his love and mercy we become part of his body, the church of Jesus Christ, seeking to be a truly redemptive community within the world.

The first and primary function or ministry of the church is the worship of God our maker. Without this, all else is of little value, for it is through worship that we learn to commune with God and find the power to do the will of God. Our sights are set, so to speak, as we learn to worship rightly. John 4:23-24 tells us "the hour is coming, and now is, when the true worshipers will worship the Father in Spirit and truth, for such the Father seeks to worship him. God is spirit, and those who worship God must worship in spirit and truth."

Every worship service should bring one into personal communion with God. The entire service is offered up as an offering unto God. The minister is supposed to be an instrument in the hand of God, through whom God's message is preached. All are responsible for the response made to God and for presenting acceptable worship unto him. True worship brings the believer into right relationship with God and presents the claims of God to both the believer and the unbeliever.

You already have a reverent worship service here, and one ought always to enter into the presence of God with a sense of awe and expectancy. God said to Moses, "Take off your shoes from your feet for the place whereon you stand is Holy Ground." Whenever people meet God, they stand on holy ground, for the place of encounter is made sacred by the presence of God and not for any other reason. Jesus facing the tempter in the wilderness said, "You shall worship the Lord your God, and him only shall you serve." Worship draws us into communion with God and away from the things of the world that are so much a part of us. Having regained our perspective week by week, we are prepared to serve God more acceptably with all of our lives. We cannot serve God properly without worshiping God. You need to remember that we are not serving the minister; you are not actually serving the church—you are serving God, and anything less than this is idolatry. So let us truly worship that we may truly serve.

Secondly, the church is to proclaim the gospel—the proclamation of Jesus Christ as Lord and Savior is its mission in the world. Do not ever forget that the gospel is proclaimed both by the pulpit and the pew; it is a shared responsibility. Both by word and deed we proclaim the riches of God and what he has done for us, or else we fail to do so. As Paul said, "We preach not ourselves, but Jesus Christ and him crucified. It is by the foolishness of preaching that God has chosen to redeem people. It is through the mystery of preaching that his message is to be heard. Of the early disciples it was said that 'every day in the temple and at home they did not cease teaching and preaching Jesus as the Christ'" (Acts 5:42). Today with a trained ministry, we often overlook the equally important role of laymen and women. Whenever the church has made a great impact upon the world, it has been when the laity has taken Jesus Christ seriously. You see, we Baptists believe in the priesthood of all believers—so each one of us has an important place to fill and is responsible to God for how we fill it.

Closely associated with the preaching ministry of the church is the teaching ministry. In fact, the two are usually coupled together. There are only a few references made to Jesus as a preacher in the New Testament. Most frequently he is referred to as a teacher. The Great Commission includes the admonition to teach them all things that he commanded. One of the great arms of the church is its teaching ministry, as you well know. Teaching spiritual truth is a slow process, but the New Testament makes it abundantly clear that Christians are meant to grow until they attain the maturity that one has the right to expect of full-grown Christians. One of the saddest things throughout the churches in America is how many of our members are content to remain babes in Christ, never having grown through all the years in association with the church.

The Scripture that we read this morning indicates that there are in the church various gifts—not all of us have the same gift, but all of us are to use whatever gift is ours for the upbuilding of the body of Christ until we all attain that degree of maturity that ought to be ours. It is a lifelong process, to be sure, and there is no end to the growth that is possible for the one who wants to grow up into the stature of the fullness of Christ. Our goal is to become like him. The disciples who walked and talked with him as he walked the earth were slow learners, but by the grace of God, they made it, and so can we.

Growth is involved in the life of the Christian and in the life of the church. The mission of the church cannot be fulfilled without it. Paul declares in Colossians 1:28, "Him we proclaim, warning everyone and teaching everyone in all wisdom, that we may present every person mature in Christ." This is the goal toward which we strive both for ourselves and for others.

Lastly, the church has the responsibility of ministering to the needs of people, whether those people are nearby or around the world, for the ministry and mission of the church is worldwide. The church is committed to do something about the sufferings and injustices in our world. We indeed have a healing ministry, reaching out to bind up the wounds of the afflicted, the oppressed, the sick, the rejected, and the lonely, for the love of Christ includes all people. If the church is to perform his healing ministry in the world today, it must be concerned with all those who need help in any way. It is interesting that Jesus said to his disciples, "Greater things than these shall you do because I go to the Father." What a statement to make, for how could anyone do anything greater than Jesus? Perhaps he meant that the combined efforts of Christians could provide more hospitals, build more missions and schools, relieve the sufferings and hurts of more people than it was possible for Jesus to do confined to one little corner of the world. By joining hands with other Christians concerned with all these needs, we express the love of Jesus Christ for a world that is very much in need of God and the love God shares through his son. God uses people like us to accomplish his purposes in the world.

The true church of Christ is made up of those who serve others in the name of Jesus Christ. "Inasmuch as you have done it unto the least of these, you have done it unto me" (Matt 25:40). This is the example and foundation of the church—to serve a needy world spiritually, mentally, physically, or however else the needs of people may be met.

If we are to fulfill our ministry, we must live a life worthy of the calling to which we have been called, and this involves each one of us, for we are called into the body of Christ to help fulfill his ministry in the world today.

"For the Son of man came not to be ministered unto but to minister and to give his life a ransom for many." This is the foundation of the church. The church at worship, the church proclaiming the gospel, the church fulfilling its teaching ministry, and the church caring for the world that needs God most of all. This is *our* ministry!

"The Ministry of the Church" was preached at First Baptist Church, Readsboro, Vermont, on Sunday, August 30, 1964. Addie had been called by the church in June 1964 and ordained on August 9, 1964, by Watts Street Baptist Church, Durham, North Carolina. She officially began her pastoral ministry at First Baptist, Readsboro, the following Sunday, but on August 30, she filled the pulpit and preached "The Ministry of the Church," her first sermon to her new congregation.

Chapter Three

R and R
(Exodus 20:8-11)

Karen Hatcher

*2010 Recipient of the
Addie Davis Award for
Excellence in Preaching*

It is not your imagination. A 2001 study conducted by the United Nations International Labor Organization confirms that United States workers put in more hours than any other industrialized nation—interesting, given that the trend elsewhere in the world is to spend *less* time on the job.[1] In his 2003 book, *The Importance of Being Lazy: In Praise of Play, Leisure and Vacations,* Al Gini of Loyola University explores Americans' obsession with work. He quotes the research of economist Juliet Schor, whose findings include the fact that annual hours on the job across all industries and occupations have been increasing over the last two decades. The average employee is now working an additional 163 hours per year—the equivalent of an extra month—with 12 percent of all full-time personnel toiling away 60-plus hours per week. In 1994, Management guru Charles Hardy reported that the typical American worker was at it 47 hours a week, or 2,330 hours annually. In 2003, he estimated that the total hours would rise to 3,000 by the year 2014. The International Labor Organization study supports the 1999 findings of a team at Cornell, which revealed that on average, Americans work 350 hours per year more than Europeans and 70 hours more than the Japanese, whose language actually has a word meaning "death by overwork."[2]

Thanks to advances in technology, we now have the option of working wherever and whenever we like, with the result that we are expected to be available to our bosses and clients around the clock. Labor market economist Lawrence Jeff Johnson, who headed up the ILO project, notes the blurring of boundaries between work and play. "I [recently] played golf on [a] Sunday with a friend of mine, the vice president of a telecommunications firm," he remarked. "His phone rang three times, all work-related." We take working lunches and working vacations. Is it any wonder that the relentless activity and chronic stress of the workplace leave us physically and emotionally exhausted? The old adage "no rest for the weary" seems distressingly descriptive of the American workforce.

This harried lifestyle leaves me feeling a bit like the Energizer bunny, but I suspect that even that hare's batteries eventually run down. In a typical week, we recharge the panoply of gadgets—everything from cell phones and cameras to iPods and laptops, even our hybrid cars. Down at the Loft Mountain Wayside where I work, we always have a visitor or two in search of an electrical outlet. We are religious about plugging these devices into a power source on a regular basis, but we rarely think about *unplugging ourselves* from the perpetual activities that deplete our own energy. Just the other day I stopped by the McDonald's in Elkton, and after ordering a hamburger, I settled into a quiet corner and promptly converted it into a mini-office. As I pulled out my cell phone and booted up my computer, a plaque hanging on the wall caught my attention. It was a dictionary entry for the word "relax": "v. 1. To make less tense or rigid; 2. To relieve from nervous stress; 3. To seek rest or recreation; 4. To cease working; to cast off anxiety." The irony left me shaking my head.

The psalmist has some sage advice for a workaholic culture: "It is useless to rise early and go to bed late, and work your worried fingers to the bone. Do not you know [God] enjoys giving rest to those he loves?" (Ps 127:2, *The Message*). The solution to the Rat Race, the R and R that is slowly killing us, is another kind of R and R—a bit of rest and relaxation.

The Hebrews called it Sabbath, a word derived from a verb meaning "to cease." The commandment to "remember the Sabbath day, to keep it holy" is the fourth listed in the Decalogue, the "ten words" given by God at Sinai to the Israelites, who had been chosen to enter into covenant relationship with the Holy One. Only a short time earlier, they had been slaving away 24-7 for Pharaoh in Egypt. Having liberated them from the oppressive working conditions, Yahweh set about forming them into a holy people whose character and conduct mirrored that of their new overlord. With Yahweh as boss, they were to observe a six-day workweek, following the pattern established at creation: "For in six days the LORD made heaven and earth, the sea and all that is in them, but rested the seventh day" (Exod 20:11). The writer of Deuteronomy gives a second reason for ceasing their labor— to allow their servants to rest, too. "Remember that you were a slave in the land of Egypt and that the LORD your God brought you out from there" (Deut 5:15). Sabbath-keeping thus served as a reminder of God's role in both creation and Israel's history. It became a distinguishing mark of the Jewish community and set them apart as distinct from the surrounding Gentile cultures throughout the centuries.

Judging from multiple references in the Old Testament narratives, God clearly included rest in the rhythm of creation. A case in point is the provision of manna during the Israelites' wilderness wandering. The strange bread would fall from heaven day by day, with a double portion on the sixth; the disobedient who went out to gather it on the Sabbath found none. God had ordered a cosmic shutdown. As Walter Brueggemann puts it, even heaven's bakeries were closed on the day of rest.[3]

In Exodus 23, we find the commandment among the laws that were to govern the fledgling nation, restated with a wider scope: "For six years you shall sow your land and gather in its yield, but the seventh year you shall let it rest and lie fallow. . . . For six days you shall do your work, but on the seventh day you shall rest so that your ox and your donkey may have relief, and your home-born slave and the resident alien may be refreshed" (vv. 10-12). The divinely ordained respite is to extend not only to human beings but also to beasts of burden and the land they cultivated. The Jews apparently failed to apply Sabbath principles to the land, for in describing the forced exile of the Jews in the sixth century BCE, the writer of 2 Chronicles observes that during the Babylonian captivity, the land was able to catch up on its Sabbath rests: "All the days that it lay desolate it kept sabbath to fulfill seventy years" (36:21).

The land that comprises Shenandoah National Park has experienced a similar regeneration during the past seventy-five years. Family farms eventually returned to forests, which were allowed to go through their natural cycle of growth, death, and decay. With all aspects of habitat protected by law, flora and fauna flourished. Wildlife sightings by early visitors to the park were generally limited to squirrels, chipmunks, rabbits, and skunks. Today, the thirteen deer originally found in the southern section number in the thousands, and around 500 black bears have taken up residence here. The lush, thriving ecosystem provides refuge not only for animals but also for us humans.

Though it was never stated in so many words, our national parks seem to have been established on Sabbath principles. In the early twentieth century, conservationist John Muir was working diligently with Washington politicos to bring the "traditional western park experience" to the urbanites of the east. His rationale was this: "Thousands of tired, nerve-shaken, over-civilized people are beginning to find that going to the mountains is going home; that wilderness is a necessity; and that mountain parks are useful, not only as fountains of timber and irrigating rivers, but as fountains of life."[4] Two decades later, Franklin D. Roosevelt echoed that sentiment in a speech dedicating Shenandoah National Park: "with the smell of the woods and the wind in the trees, they will forget the rush and the strain of all the other long weeks of the year, and for a short time at least, the days will be good for their hearts and good for their souls."[5] So the park's *raison d'être* is, in FDR's words, R and R—"for the recreation and the re-creation" visitors will find here.[6] Perhaps you, too, have found this place to be a recharging station, where our batteries can truly be reenergized by the divine power that per-meates these premises. Having willfully disengaged from the workplace and dislocated ourselves to a woodland wilderness, we can hope to enjoy the physical and spiritual renewal described by John Muir:

> Climb the mountains and get their good tidings.
> Nature's peace will flow into you as sunlight into trees.
> The winds will blow their own freshness into you
> And the storms their energy,
> While cares drop off like autumn leaves.[7]

The beauty of Shenandoah promotes our ability to enter into the Sab-bath experience to which our Lord summons us. I am reminded of Psalm 23:2-3, where the natural setting also plays a key role in replenishing our depleted reserves: "He makes me lie down in green pastures; he leads me beside the still waters. He restores my soul." In *The Message,* Eugene Peterson puts it this way: "You have bedded me down in lush meadows; you find me quiet pools to drink from. True to your word, you let me catch my breath." Significantly, it is in the outdoors that God breathes new life into the psalmist, and he is able to find refreshment for his *soul.* The word for "soul" in the Old Testament writings—*nephesh*—refers to one's entire being, reflect-ing the Hebrews' more holistic understanding. Here the psalmist is affirming God's ability to restore the whole person. At the end of the workweek, we are called to lay aside the incessant human doing and become human beings, being still for a while and knowing that the Lord is God.

Perhaps in your experience, Sabbath represents another kind of R and R—rules and regulations, restrictive prohibitions that made the day of rest a burden rather than a blessing and distorted the purpose of Sabbath observance. From the perspective of the Gospel writers, Jesus' life-restoring Sabbath labors seemed more threatening than therapeutic to some of the religious authorities of his day. But our Lord not only modeled the true meaning of Sabbath—he was and is its source. This is his invitation: "Are you tired? Worn out? Burned out on religion? Come to me. Get away with me, and you will recover your life. I will show you how to take a real rest. Walk with me and work with me—watch how I do it. Learn the unforced rhythms of grace" (Matt 11:28-29, *The Message*).

Among the secrets to finding rest for our souls is Sabbath-keeping. Admittedly, this takes more than a dash of discipline, especially with our over-packed schedules. But the Creator-boss we serve hit the pause button at the end of a very busy workweek, and invites—even insists—that we go and do likewise. It is the divine intent during this brief time of recreation to re-create us by renewing our minds, renewing a right spirit within us, and renewing our strength so that we can soar like eagles. This is God's idea of R and R—Respite and Reflection—downtime spent contemplating and enjoying the One who is continually revitalizing creation. It is an offer we can't refuse: "Come to me, O weary traveler; come to me, with your distress; come to me, you heavy burdened; come to me and find your rest. Rest in me, O weary traveler, rest in me and do not fear. Rest in me, my heart is gentle; rest and cast away your care."[8] Let us get into the habit of punching out once a week on the cosmic time clock like the rest of creation. After all, it is corporate policy.

"R and R" was preached at Loft Mountain Amphitheater, Shenandoah National Park, Virginia, on Sunday, June 24, 2012.

Notes

1. Porter Anderson, "Study: U.S. Employees Put in Most Hours," CNN Career, 31 August 2001.

2. Al Gini, *The Importance of Being Lazy: In Praise of Play, Leisure and Vacations* (New York: Routledge, 2003) 15–16.

3. Walter Brueggemann, *The New Interpreter's Bible*, vol. 1 (Nashville: Abingdon Press, 1994) 814.

4. John Muir, 1914, quoted in *Shenandoah Overlook*, Summer 2012, 1.

5. Franklin Roosevelt, speech at Shenandoah National Park Dedication Ceremony, 3 July 1936, quoted in *Oh, Ranger! Guide to Shenandoah National Park*, Summer 2011, 12.

6. Ibid., 1.

7. John Muir, *Our National Parks* (New York: Houghton, Mifflin and Company, 1901) 56.

8. Sylvia Dunstan, "Come to Me, O Weary Traveler," 1990, *Chalice Hymnal* (St. Louis, MO: Chalice Press, 1995) 353.

Chapter Four

Catching a Glimpse

Dear Glee
Thank you for
all you do to
make Baptist Women
proud.
Kim
Schmitt
Holman

(Numbers 27:1-11; Luke 8:1-3)

Kimberly Schmitt Holman

2000 Recipient of the Addie Davis Award for Excellence in Preaching

In the book of Numbers, we can spend some time in the company of five sisters who stand in a line of men in the hot sun, looking for answers from their God. And the answers the sisters received surprised even Moses.

At this point in the book of Numbers, the Hebrew people are in the wilderness. They have been there for roughly thirty-eight years, and they have had some hard times. The journey from Egypt to Canaan should have only taken them ten days, but for some mysterious reason, the Israelites needed several years more to complete the journey. Perhaps their experience was a little like being in grade school, where if you are not ready to move to the next level, the teacher will hold you back. If that analogy is true, the Hebrews got held back thirty-nine times, and they may have been the slowest learners ever. They had been given commandments; they broke the commandments. They had followed God through pillars of cloud and torches of fire; they rebelled against God. The latest rebellion in a long line of Hebrew rebellions was led by a fellow named Korah, who decided that Moses should not be their leader anymore. Korah gathered up people who thought like him, and together they tried to kick Moses out. But getting rid of Moses was a little harder than getting rid of an employee who is no longer pulling her load. Moses was God's chosen liberator, and God was not done with Moses. Even so, Korah started an uprising, seeking to unseat Moses, and God was not happy. In Numbers 16, we read that Korah and his rebellious army were swallowed up in the ground for their insubordination.

Time moved on. The Hebrew people were finally ready to move into the promised land. But before they could begin the last leg of their journey, a census had to be taken. The reason for this census was an important one. The information gathered would be used to decide how much land each family received once they entered the promised land. So the census taking began, and each "man" was to come forward and tell Moses about the size of his family so that land could be appropriated for that family.

But a scandal soon would unfold. As the line formed early on the appointed morning, five women stood huddled together waiting for their turn to see Moses. I am sure that the women heard whispers and saw pointing fingers. I am sure that some of the men behind them in line urged these five women to move aside, informing them not all that politely that they should not waste Moses' valuable time. Perhaps other people simply sadly shook their heads, because they knew of the story of these poor women. You see, these women, Mahlah, Noah, Hoglah, Milcah, and Tirzah, were sisters. Their father had died. They had no brothers. None of them were married. There was no "man" to stand in line for their family, and there was absolutely no way for them to take care of themselves if Moses refused what they were about to ask him.

Finally, the women's turn came. The five sisters approached Moses, probably a little fearful, since his answer would be the difference between their livelihood and their destitution. One sister spoke up: "Our father died in the wilderness. He was not one of the ones who rebelled against the LORD in the company of Korah. He died for his own sin, and he had no son. Why should the name of our father be erased from his clan because he had no son? Give to us a possession among our father's brothers" (Num 27:3-4).

I imagine that Moses was speechless. He does not say a word to the five sisters. He just stares for a moment, turns and goes into the tent, and takes this case directly to God. Moses knows that whatever the outcome will be, he does not want to be blamed for mishandling it. So Moses asks God about the sisters' request, and God appears to decide fairly quickly. God agrees with the daughters and says to Moses, "You shall indeed let them possess an inheritance with their father's brothers and pass the inheritance of their father along to them" (Num 27:7). In fact, God makes a new law for Israel as a result of this encounter. If there are no sons, God declares that daughters should inherit the family property, and if there are no daughters, then the property goes to the man's brother, then to his father's brothers, then to his nearest kinsman. Finally, women have a place in the chain of inheritance.

When I first heard this story, it was told in support of the equality of women. The preacher reminded her congregation that women deserve to have their voices heard, and in some cases, women must demand to be heard, just like Mahlah, Noah, Hoglah, Milcah, and Tirzah did. And the preacher is indeed right. Women do need to find places to express themselves, and they need to be heard.

But this story is not just about women's liberation and women's equality. This story, in fact, does not offer much to the feminist movement. Even after Moses speaks this new law into existence, women were in no way equal to men; women were still second-class citizens. After all, wives are nowhere to be found in the chain of inheritance. And daughters only were to receive an inheritance *if* their fathers had no sons. Sure, this law was a step in the right direction, but it did not bring about women's equality.

I think this story has a lesson that is even more powerful. These five sisters saw something wrong with the way their society worked, and rather than accepting the injustice, they attempted to change it. Rather than wail about the unfairness of life, the women rose up early in the morning and got in line to have a talk with Moses. And getting a chance to talk to Moses was a bit like marching onto the White House lawn and demanding to speak to the president, hoping the Secret Service will not arrest you. After all, these sisters knew all about Korah. Remember what happened to him. When he and his minions rebelled against Moses, God opened the ground beneath them and let it swallow them up. That would give anyone pause. Given Korah's experience, I am not sure I would mess with Moses. But these women were gutsy, and we have a lot to learn from them.

In the book of Joshua, we hear about these sisters again. In that story, some of their relatives express fear that these sisters will marry outside of their clan and that the family's land that was given to them could be taken over by another Israelite clan. Joshua responds by issuing a decree that the sisters must marry within their own clan. Over the years, rabbis continue to tell a story about the sisters. It is not found in the Scriptures, but the story is that these five women would not marry until they found just the right man, and even though each of the five waited a long time to marry, they conceived and had sons. They were gutsy to the end.

Ever since my seminary days, when I was first introduced to these five sisters, I have often felt a kinship with them. They were women who chose to speak up, to speak up to God and Moses, to speak up in the presence of all of Israel, and to speak about something that was not right. They did not do it with finger pointing. They did not do it with pleas, pouting, or tears. They did not do it with yells of outrage. They went to the one person who could solve their problem, and they asked for help. Moses then did his part by relaying the message, and God did what we know God does. God advocated for women in a time and in a society that did not always hold women's rights as a matter of course.

While what these daughters did was bold, they did it not to make headlines. They did it instead because they needed Moses and God to hear of their plight. This story is remembered and preserved in Scripture, and today, in reading the story, we remember that women can make a difference in the world. Ordinary women can make a difference by asking good questions and finding out who can best help. Five women step up to make the world a better place for themselves and for the women who will follow them. They are only five of many people, men and women, but they worked to make our world a better, more just place.

Too often the stories of women get left out. If we look closely, we can catch a glimpse of these sisters. But let's be honest. The reason most people do not know about this great story in Numbers is that we get so bored by all the numbers, the census taking, and the "who begat whom" that we never really look to see what treasures we might find in this book of the Bible. If we look closely, we catch a glimpse.

In Luke's Gospel, three short verses remind us too that not all of Jesus' followers were men. When we think of the followers of Jesus, we normally think of the disciples, the twelve men that Jesus chose to be fishers with him of human beings. If we work hard together, we might even be able to give names to all twelve. But in Luke 8:1-3, we read of some other people who followed Jesus, people who are often overlooked:

> Soon afterward, Jesus went on through cities and villages, proclaiming and bringing the good news of the kingdom of God. The twelve were with him, as well as some women who had been cured of evil spirits and infirmities: Mary, called Magdalene, from whom seven demons had gone out, and Joanna, the wife of Herod's steward, Chuza, and Susanna, and many others who provided for them out of their resources.

Have you ever thought about how Jesus was able to meet his basic needs? Sure, according to the temptation story, Jesus had the power to turn stones into bread, but we know that Jesus refused to do that. We know that he did make seven loaves and a few fish feed a crowd of five thousand men plus the women and children. We have read that Jesus ate at the tables of saints and sinners, but I do not imagine he had a place there every night. What we do not hear about Jesus or his disciples doing is working, earning money. In the book of Acts, we read about Paul taking his trade on the road, using his tent-making skills to meet his material needs. But in the Gospels we never read about Jesus picking up a hammer and seeking employment. We do not learn about Peter, James, John, or Andrew going out fishing and then selling their fish in the market for profit. What we do read here in Luke's account is that there were women following Jesus who provided for his needs and the disciples' needs out of their own pockets.

And who are these women? This account is the only mention of Mary Magdalene when she was not at the cross or the tomb. We know that she was not a prostitute as one of the early church fathers labeled her. She was a woman who followed Jesus because he healed her of seven demons that possessed her body, and even though we may not believe in demons today, we know that there was something terribly wrong with her, and Jesus fixed it. In response, she decided to follow and support him.

Luke includes the name of Joanna, the wife of Chuza, Herod's steward. She could have been someone who was seen as the enemy, but instead she followed Jesus and provided for him. We do not know Joanna's story, but perhaps she too had been cured or healed. The only time the name Susanna is mentioned in the Bible is here in Luke's Gospel. All we know of Susanna is that she and *many* other women followed Jesus too. They were the reason Jesus and the disciples did not have to worry about finding food. They were the reason Jesus never had to beg. They were the reason Jesus was able to concentrate on his ministry of helping and healing others.

I imagine that these women were the reason that Jesus was safe for as long as he was from the Pharisees and the Roman authorities. As Chuza's wife, Joanna probably had a little political clout. After all, Chuza was Herod's steward, and in those days, a Roman steward was a close advisor. Jesus may well have been saved from Herod many times by Joanna's intervention until that fateful day when Pilate decided that keeping the peace could come with a man's life as the price tag.

Behind the scenes, only noted as a transition into a bigger story, the women in Numbers and in Luke worked to make the world a better place. The five sisters stood up and asked why. The women followers of Jesus supported him so that he could do his good work, God's work, without having to worry about money. Women made the difference—even if their stories were mostly back stage. Think what we could do if we were to stand up to all the "Moseses" of the world and tell them that something is not right. Think of the good we can do by supporting others in their personal good works and in following Christ ourselves. Sometimes we will feel like our efforts are in vain. But we also know and trust that we have a God who stands behind us and before us, who works in our hearts and in the hearts of others to make things right, a God who extends peace and love into the world. If we work quietly, behind the scenes, in the small ways we have available to us, how might we be able to change the world?

There is a story about a mother who wished to encourage her young son's progress at the piano. She bought tickets for a performance by Ignace Paderewski, the famous Polish concert pianist. When the night arrived, the mother and son found their seats near the front of the concert hall and eyed the majestic Steinway waiting on stage. Soon the mother found a friend to talk with, and while she was distracted, her son slipped away. When eight o'clock arrived, the spotlights came on, and the audience quieted. And there on the stage sat the young boy on the piano stool, innocently picking out "Twinkle, Twinkle, Little Star." His mother gasped, but before she could retrieve her son, Paderewski appeared on stage and moved to the piano.

"Don't quit—keep playing," he whispered to the boy. Leaning over, Paderewski reached down with his left hand and began filling in a bass part. Soon his right arm reached around the other side, encircling the child, to add a running obligato. Together, the old master and the young novice held the crowd mesmerized.[1]

In our lives, unpolished though we may be, it is God, our master, who surrounds us and whispers in our ear, time and again, "Don't quit—keep playing." And as we keep playing, God augments and supplements until a work of amazing beauty is created—just as God did in the lives of these mostly unknown women in Numbers and Luke's Gospel. May God help us, in all that we do, to be people who in big and small ways change the world around us for the better. Amen.

Note

1. "A Little Boy at a Big Piano," author unknown, http://www.inspirationpeak.com/shortstories/bigpiano.html (accessed 30 January 2014).

Chapter Five

Lee, You are perfectly gifted! Angela D.

God's Greatest Gift

(Joshua 1:1-9)

Angela Fields

*2012 Recipient of the Addie Davis
Award for Outstanding Leadership
in Pastoral Ministry*

"Visionary," "prophet," and "futurist thinker" are all words associated with a leader. We read books that tell us a leader is to be a risk-taker with ambition and a persuasive demeanor. We rarely hear leaders described as obedient, faithful, or "second-best," but today's text is about a leader who was obedient, faithful, and, yes, "second-best."

Joshua 1 is a familiar passage that describes God's promotion of Joshua from Moses' intern to leader of the Hebrew people. As someone who once served as an intern, I can relate to Joshua. I was an intern for Nickelodeon in New York City, and I remember all the crazy tasks I was assigned: making coffee runs, logging hours of video footage, and listening to audiotapes to locate the perfect set of tire-screeching noises. I once even had to scour the streets of Manhattan on the coldest night of the winter in search of a cactus. Despite the sometimes-tedious assignments, I learned much about television production from the staff at Nickelodeon.

As Moses' intern, I can only imagine what kinds of duties Joshua was given, but the book bearing his name lets us know that Joshua learned much during his internship. But we all know that the test of how successful an intern is comes when he has to strike out on his own, when she gets her first leadership position.

If we circle around the words in the text, it has a sneaky way of telling us how Joshua's internship actually groomed him for leadership. In Joshua 1:1, the young man is described as a servant, a word that denotes obedience. The Merriam-Webster dictionary defines obedience as having a sphere of jurisdiction. In the Greek, "sphere" is *sphaira,* which means globe or something that is perfectly round. By playing with these words a bit, we can conclude that before God promoted Joshua to the top leadership role, God shaped the young man, fashioning him into a well-rounded leader. Another way we can look at *servant* is to understand it to mean *minister,* which is how the Amplified Version translates this word. Joshua was a minister, and he had a heart to serve others, to minister to those around him. The best leaders are those who desire to serve, to minister.

We have all lived through long election seasons in which we have listened to exaggerated rhetoric and fervent speeches that tell us why we should choose this person or that person. I am not usually impressed, but occasionally an eloquent speech strikes me—especially if it focuses on thoughtful policies that aim to help others rather than centering on the attempt to get the politician elected. We all know that the best leaders have a passion for serving others. We know that leaders who are selfless rather than selfish inspire us, that we are drawn to them. According to our text, Joshua was a selfless leader, and he was exactly the kind of leader that God needed for the divine task that lay ahead.

Our text tells us that Joshua, this servant leader, is chosen by God following the death of Moses, and in the moment of his selection, Joshua is also given his divine marching orders. In my ministry circle, we refer to this as "the shift," which is a reference to God moving things around. The shift is when the least becomes the greatest, when the tail becomes the head, when the last is before the first. Again, Scripture has a sneaky way of introducing us to Joshua's shift. We know Moses's story. He was a man who had lived like a prince, who had tasted royalty, but our text tells us that Joshua was the son of Nun. We know that Nun is a reference to his family—Nun was perhaps his father's name or his tribal name. But what if we play a bit with the word. Perhaps Joshua was the son of "none." Perhaps he came from nothing, as we would say. Maybe his was a broken home or no home at all. He might have been financially challenged, underappreciated, and not well educated, but God chose him. God used him, and the same is true for us. Our background does not determine how God will use us. God can move us past brokenness, poverty, the lack of education. God can elevate us to lofty places despite our circumstances.

I am one of fourteen children, born to parents who received no more than a middle school education. My childhood neighborhood was crime-ridden and dangerous. Most who lived there did not value education. They simply lived in survival mode. So for me, the thought of earning more than a high school diploma never crossed my mind. I had no thoughts of going to college, much less graduate school. But today, with God's help, I have both a bachelor's degree and a Master of Divinity degree. God took me from "nothing" and put people and opportunities in my path so that I could study and learn. God opened doors of education to me. In my heart, I know that God has provided these opportunities so that I can help lead a new generation of believers.

Joshua too was called to lead the new generation. In Joshua 1:5-6, God commissioned the new Hebrew leader to do three things: (1) to lead the people into the promised land, (2) to defeat the unknown enemies of the land, and (3) to claim their inheritance. So Joshua is told of his responsibility. But this is where life gets a little hairy. While God commissioned Joshua and assigned him these tasks, God did not give Joshua a detailed road map or comprehensive instructions as to how to accomplish his new duties. God did not tell Joshua how long the assignment would take to complete. God did, however, let Joshua know that he would have a fight on his hands. Now come closer, I want to tell you a secret. Come a little closer. Sometimes it takes a long time and a lot of fighting to receive the fullness of what God has for you. Remember Joshua had already been wandering in the wilderness with the people of Israel for forty years. He had been serving Moses for a long time. He had been groomed for years to be a leader. But he still will have to fight if he follows God's calling. The work has just begun. And the lesson for us, of course, is that we will not receive our "promised land" without doing the work, staying on course, fighting the good fight. We still have work to do.

In Joshua 1:3, God promises Joshua that every place his foot treads will be given unto the Hebrew people: "I will give it to your descendants." In the Hebrew language, "every place your foot should tread" is in the imperfect tense, which signifies future actions. But the verb "give" or *natan* is in perfect tense and signifies past events or actions. A careful reading of this verse tells us that before the battle starts, God has already determined the winner. God knows the outcome.

Our response, like Joshua's response, is to be strong and courageous, to meditate on the word of God, and to live and lead in accordance to God's law. In Hebrew, one meaning of the word "meditate" is "mutter." The Jewish people, in reading the Torah, often muttered the words to themselves, repeating them over and over (Deut 6:6-9). So when we read Joshua 1:8, in which Joshua was told to "always keep the Book of the Law on your lips," we know that God intended for him never to stop speaking God's words, to repeat them over and over to himself. Such a practice not only brings to mind God's word but also allows God to speak and to guide. Like Joshua, we need to be meditating, muttering the words given to us by God, repeating the Scripture to ourselves over and over again, and thereby allow God to speak to us.

Like Joshua, we are called to trust God's promises and to step out in faith, and when we do, we can be sure that the Lord will give us guidance, maybe not specific directions, but the guidance we need. We also know that on our journey, we can gain strength and courage from God's word. But perhaps the most important thing to remember, the greatest gift we have, is the knowledge that along the way, God will be with us. For the Lord promises never to leave us or forsake us on our journey. We, as God's people, can move forward and be assured of God's divine presence. We can be confident in the assurance that God will be with us as we journey across our Jordan Rivers and move into a new land. Amen.

Chapter Six

Where Love Abides

(Joshua 24:1-2, 14-15; John 6:56-69; Psalm 84)

Nicole Finkelstein-Blair

2001 Recipient of the Addie Davis
Award for Excellence in Preaching

As a little girl, Finn would spend sum-
mers at her grandmother's house in the
small-town heat of Grasse, California. Wearing cut-off jean shorts and long
pigtails, she would seek a bit of cool wherever she could find it: at the local
pool, with an icy glass of lemonade, or under the large rectangle of shade
created by the quilt-in-progress that stretched across a wooden frame,
belonging to her grandmother's quilting circle.

Sitting there, sipping her lemonade, looking up at the underside of the
quilt, Finn spent those hot summer days watching the quilters' nimble fingers press needles in and out of the layers of fabric and listening to the
women tease, advise, laugh, and tell stories. Their tales were pieced as intri-
cately as snippets of fabric. Their lives were bound together as firmly as the
coziest coverlet.

That scene, a little girl shaded under the quilt and surrounded by the
women whose fingers created that shelter, stitch by stitch, is the beginning
of the book *How to Make an American Quilt.*[1] But little girls cannot stay
little forever, and Finn grows up. In time, the women gather again around
a quilt frame to piece together Finn's wedding quilt. Once again, they work
to create a kind of shelter and comfort for her. Once again, their stories surround her. For this special quilt, each of the women makes a single square

that represents her own story and her wish for Finn's new marriage. When all their blocks—all their stories—are bound together, they name the quilt "Where Love Abides." Together their blocks tell the story of abiding love. Individual blocks tell of lifelong relationships, heartbreak and hearts mended, slavery and freedom, family, loss, and new life. Each square of fabric is a story, a word of encouragement, a lesson for life together, reflections on the relationships that shaped the past and present, and a challenge for the new couple's future.

Joshua 24 tells the story of the very last chapters of Joshua's life. This great leader of God's people gathered the community in a place called Shechem, the place where God had once gifted Abraham with the promised land. Abraham had built an altar at Shechem, and it became the first place of worship in the land of promise. Surrounded by the landmarks of their history, Joshua called the people together in the presence of their leaders and elders, and he began to preach.

In this place set apart by God, a place where they could not help but see the story of God's care for them reflected in the sites of their ancestors and in the faces of their leaders, Joshua pieced together the story like strips of cloth—from Father Abraham to the enslavement in Egypt to the wilderness to the promised land. The narrative surrounded them, stories of God's lifelong love of the people, stories of heartbreak and redemption, stories of slavery and freedom. Stories of the family of tribes, stories of loss, stories of finding new life in the long-awaited land. Joshua stitched together these words of encouragement, lessons for life together, reflections on the relationship with their Creator, who shaped their past and present. And he gave a challenge for the people's future:

> Now therefore revere the LORD, and serve him in sincerity and faithfulness; put away the gods that your ancestors served beyond the River and in Egypt, and serve the LORD. Now if you are unwilling to serve the LORD, choose this day whom you will serve . . . but as for me and my household, we will serve the LORD. (Joshua 24:14-15)

Like Joshua, Jesus liked to piece stories together. He liked to surround the people with real-life, walking-around stories of God's love and caretaking. John's Gospel sets up the frame and stretches the fabric across it, displaying the images of Jesus turning water into wine, Jesus telling the lame man to stand up and walk, Jesus portioning out a few fish and loaves to feed a hungry crowd, Jesus stepping out onto the water when the storms raged, and Jesus retelling the ancient tales of God's provision in the wilderness.

In his stories, Jesus surrounded the people with words of encouragement, lessons for life together, and reflections on their relationship with the One who was their past and their present. Then in the sixth chapter of John's Gospel, Jesus began to piece together a new Story, a Story that was his own, a Story that was his very Self. He told them the Story of bread that is abiding love, bread that is eternal life. He told them that they could be part of that Story, be part of him. They could partake of the bread of his body and be part of the love that indwells. They could be part of the life that never ends. Then Jesus gave them the challenge for their future:

> "The words that I have spoken to you are spirit and life. But among you there are some who do not believe." And he said, "For this reason I have told you that no one can come to me unless it is granted by the Father." Because of this many of his disciples turned back and no longer went about with him. So Jesus asked the twelve, "Do you also wish to go away?" (John 6:67)

Here in the church, we too are quilters, piecing together our story as people of God. Like children huddled in the shadow of the quilt frame, we listen to our elders talk and laugh. We listen to them tell their tales, soaking those stories in, learning how we should be, and growing slowly but surely under their watchful eyes. Like the children of Israel at Shechem, we surround ourselves with physical reminders of our journey. Instead of Abraham's altar, we gather in a sanctuary. We listen to Scripture and to song. We sit in silence. We partake of the Supper. Like the disciples listening to Jesus' teachings, we struggle to understand this Person who is the Story, even though we have seen his work among us; we ask him to explain it one more time, and once more, and just one more again.

We live in the intersection of past, present, and future. We take encouragement from the stories of the generations before us, and then we circle up around the table and tell our own parts of the story, so that the children at our feet can absorb our words. We look toward days to come, knowing we will all grow up, older and wiser and closer. We know that the roads we will travel will not be easy. But we do our best, time and again, to answer the challenge of today's faith—a challenge that has not changed over millennia: Whom will we serve? Or do we also wish to go away?

Earlier this summer, my younger son, Levi, and I drove into this church's parking lot. When we pulled into the lot, Levi looked at the homey buildings here and said, "Whose house is this?" Naturally, I summoned up all my seminary training and ministerial experience and took the opportunity to engage in a deep theological moment. . . . No, I didn't. Actually, I completely dropped the ball. When he asked, "Whose house is this?" I said something like, "Oh, honey, this is not a house. It is a church." I think these days that might be known as a "face-palm" moment.

The good news is that at least one of us learned a lesson that day. I do not think I will ever come to this church again without remembering just whose house this is, and I hope that remembering this house will help me remember the right answer in every church that we attend so that when my children ask, I will tell them what I know to be true: the church is the house of God. The church is where love abides.

Though I failed to teach it to my child that afternoon, the Scriptures are thankfully full of reminders of the joy of being part of the household of God. In Psalm 84, we read,

> How lovely is your dwelling place, O LORD of hosts!
> My soul longs, indeed it faints for the courts of the LORD;
> My heart and my flesh sing for joy to the living God.
> Happy are those who live in your house, ever singing your praise.
> For a day in your courts is better than a thousand elsewhere!

The people of God have gathered over the centuries to hear the stories that our forefathers and foremothers of faith were bursting to tell. When we have wandered, we have been led. When we have been hungry, we have been filled. When lame, we have been lifted. When alone, we have been called together, gathered up. And when we received the challenge, we have answered.

Whom will we serve? Along with the people of Israel, we answer, "The Lord our God we will serve, and him we will obey."

Do we wish to go away? Along with the apostle Simon Peter, we answer, "Lord, to whom can we go? You have the words of eternal life. We have come to believe and know that you are the Holy One of God."

As a military family, we relocate every two-and-a-half or three years. I grew up moving just as often because of my dad's job in the business world. As you might imagine, I have a bit of trouble understanding the whole concept of "abiding." Journeying and wandering—these make sense to me.

Abiding—abiding is hard. I have had days recently when I was not even sure what my home address was. One day I had to look myself up in the church directory to find my correct house number! More and more, though, I think our family is just an extreme example of a struggle that many people feel to be "at home." I have a hunch that we all have a hard time with abiding. Maybe we are not always roaming from house to house or state to state, but I think many of us have the sensation of being "strangers in a strange land." We may feel at odds with our culture. We pray, sing, and speak words of peace in a world that seems more inclined to shout, sling mud, and speak words of violence. We may feel at odds with traditional religion because we experience God working and calling in new or unorthodox ways. We may be afraid to settle down, to be here now, because we think we must stay on the defensive, ready for "fight or flight." We may feel unsure of our place because we have questions that others refuse to ask, or because we are willing to affirm that Jesus' Story is true even when we cannot explain it.

Yet when our wandering has been long and scary and difficult, we say, again and again, "We will serve the Lord, for he is our God." And when we don't feel at home in this world, we say, "Happy are those who live in your house." And when our understanding is limited by our five senses and our linear lifespan, we say, "Where else would we go? You have the words of eternal life." So for all of us who are wandering: Welcome home. There is a place here, a place where love abides, a place for you and me, a place for every questioning child—those among us and those deep inside us. There is a place at the table, where grace is spoken and shared, where we share in the body of Christ, the bread of life. And there is a place around the frame of the Story that we are piecing together, one block at a time, one stitch at a time; one laugh, one tear, one love, one life at a time.

This is our prayer today:

> You welcome us into your dwelling place, Lord,
> and you surround us with reminders of your presence.
> You fulfill your promises to us,
> and you receive our praise.
> You challenge us daily to choose your way, to serve you,
> to be at home wherever you are.
> You invite us to partake of your body
> and in doing so to become part of your eternal Story.
> Thank you for all the spiritual ancestors who have so faithfully
> stitched your love into life, so we could be sheltered in it.

Thank you, too, for all the children who find your comfort
in the work of our own hands and hearts.
Help us, your church, to piece your narrative honestly,
lovingly, wholeheartedly,
so that your image will be visible,
and your Story made known. Amen.

"Where Love Abides" was preached at Covenant Baptist Church, San Antonio, Texas, on Sunday, August 26, 2012.

Note

1. Whitney Otto, *How to Make an American Quilt* (New York: Ballentine Books, 1992).

Chapter Seven

My God
(1 Samuel 2:1-10)

Griselda Escobar

2011 Recipient of the Addie Davis Award for Outstanding Leadership in Pastoral Ministry

I remember the first time I went to Disneyland. My family had lived in Los Angeles for about a year, and my siblings and I had been waiting to go to the theme park. Going became our continual prayer request. But my parents were ministers with five kids. At the age of nine, as the oldest sibling, I was very aware of the difficulty of making a trip to Disneyland happen, and yet I often went into my room and prayed, "Lord, please, I really want to go to Disneyland." And then it happened: a miraculous answered prayer! Even today, it is one of my most memorable answered prayers. During that first trip to the theme park, I was so excited, and every time I got on a ride, I thanked God.

We all have stories of answered prayers, and we hold on to the joy we felt knowing the Lord had responded. In 1 Samuel 2, we read of Hannah, who also experienced an answered prayer. My Disneyland prayer experience in no way reflects the depth of Hannah's pain, the passion of her request. Her petition was much more important to her than mine had been to me. But the end result was the same: God answered our prayers.

You remember this story. Hannah was one of Elkanah's two wives. His other wife, Peninnah, had given him many children, but Hannah was barren. As in any story of polygamy, both women suffered in this relationship and were hurt by one another. Peninnah, knowing that even though she bore Elkanah's children, realized that he loved Hannah more than her, and out of her jealousy, Peninnah inflicted pain on Hannah, severely taunting her and belittling her. The taunting went on for years. It did not happen just once; it was an everyday struggle for Hannah.

Yet Hannah endured more than just taunting. In those days, women had no value if they could not provide their husbands with sons, and thus, Hannah believed herself to be of no value to her beloved husband. Her affliction was not just that she was infertile; she also questioned daily her value as a person, as a human being. The only dream she had in life had been taken from her.

Despite Elkanah's disappointment, he continued to live a life of faith. Year after year he traveled to Shiloh to worship and to make sacrifices, and there he offered sacrifices on behalf of his wives and children. Year after year, out of his great love for Hannah, he gave double portions on her behalf. Finally, after living with this hurt and disappointment for decades, Hannah goes into the Lord's house. She is no longer able to continue carrying her pain. She cannot live like this one more year, one more month, one more day, and she confronts God and begins negotiations. The text does not tell us if every year she prayed for a son, but we know that this year, she does. This year she goes into the Lord's house with a request, a demand, and her prayers attract attention.

"Give me one son, just one," she begs, "and I will give him back. Let me give my husband what he needs from me. Let me be valued as a person. Let me feel the joy of having a son, of caring for a child of mine." Her prayers put her pain on display, and Hannah comes to God's house with more than an offering; she brings a broken heart.

Some scholars believe that the temple in Shiloh was a place of sacrifice and that people did not visit simply to pray. Perhaps that explains why the priest, Eli, confronts Hannah and asks if she is drunk. Or perhaps Hannah's cry is so deep, so painful, that no sound comes from her moving lips, and seeing her in that condition, Eli determines that she is drunk. Yet, despite Eli's question, despite what others around her are saying, Hannah does not give them her attention. She continues in her prayers, pouring out her heart to God.

Today, we all know stories of people who are brokenhearted. There is the young newlywed couple, expecting their first baby, but who, after the first excited months of pregnancy, experience a miscarriage. Their dream, their expectation of becoming parents, and their future story of life with a child is suddenly taken. There is the woman in our neighborhood. She has been married for years, but suddenly her husband leaves her for someone else. Her heart is broken. Her dream of who they were together is shattered, and everything she once believed to be true now feels false. There is the teenage boy, the one who dreams of playing professional ball, but then he hurts his arm, and he cannot even try out for the high school team. His dream is gone. His goals die. His purpose evaporates.

All those hurting people remind us of Job. Poor Job loses everything, and at the end of the story, he begins to tell God how he feels. He pours out his pain and anger. He displays his broken heart to God. And God answers. God tells Job that God is God, that God will continue to be God, and that God has not ceased to be God even in the midst of Job's circumstances. After hearing from God, Job recognizes that he knows God as never before, and in Job 42:5, we hear Job say, "I had heard of you by the hearing of the ear, but now my eye sees you." Job marvels, "Now I know you through experience, now I have seen your glory firsthand. I know in my heart that you are God. I know you are *my* God." For Job, God becomes personal. God is no longer just the God of the ancient fathers, the God of past religions, or the God of an eschatological hope. God becomes "my God."

Like Job, when Hannah had received grace from God, she saw God in a new way. God was now "my God." God was personal. After giving birth to Samuel and later to five other children, Hannah sings to God, "My heart exults in the LORD; my strength is exalted in my God. My mouth derides my enemies, because I rejoice in my victory. There is no Holy One like the LORD, no one besides you; there is no Rock like our God" (1 Sam 2:1-2).

It is this personal God who, after you have lost a child, blesses your home with another, biological or adopted. It is this personal God who blesses your family even though you might never have children. It is this personal God who restores and heals the broken heart of infidelity. It is this personal God who calls you to be faithful and hold fast to your values even when others trample on them. It is this personal God who gives you a bigger and greater dream even though you think your hopes and dreams have been destroyed. It is this personal God. My God, our God, your God!

Norma Ruth, a fifteen-year-old girl living in Reynosa, Mexico, was diagnosed with leukemia. She received treatment and her health improved, but after a year the cancer came back. Norma Ruth was sicker than before, and she was once again hospitalized. As friends and family came to her hospital room, she told them that she knew God would heal her. Her optimism worried her mother, who talked with Norma Ruth, telling her that there was a possibility that God would not heal her, but the teenage girl replied, "Mom, God will heal me. If I get up from this bed with you, or if I am lifted up to be with the Lord, either way I will be healed." Norma Ruth was healed—

and went to be with God. But before she died, she sang this song: "Lord, You are good, your mercy is eternal, every morning as I awake, I know I have you to trust because your fidelity sustains me." Norma Ruth's God was a personal God, a God who gave strength and joy all at the same time.

Today, with Hannah and with Norma Ruth, we can pray, "My heart exults in the LORD; my strength is exalted in *my* God . . . . There is no Holy One like the LORD, no one besides you; there is no Rock like *our* God" (1 Sam 2:1-2).

Chapter Eight

Faces of God
(Psalm 46)

LeAnn Gunter Johns
*2004 Recipient of the Addie Davis
Award for Excellence in Preaching*

Where is God? Who is God? I find myself asking these questions on a fairly regular basis. "You?" you might ask. "You, a minister of the gospel, and you do not know where God is?" Yes, I, a minister of the gospel, ask these questions from time to time. Most days as I serve as a minister, I have the opportunity to study Scripture together with delightful people, many of whom have spent more time in church through the years than anywhere else. I have the opportunity to walk with people as they discover a new calling or as they hear God challenging them to do something new and different. There are times when I am called to walk alongside folks in joyous moments of life. These are the exciting times: the birth of a child, a job promotion, the blessing of a marriage. And then there are the other times, the ones that seem to happen in multiples: times of loss, sickness, separation, even perhaps times of death. I sometimes am caught off guard, surprised by these kinds of moments. I find myself asking the questions, Where is God? Who is God? What does God look like?

A few years back, in addition to my role as associate pastor at a church in Atlanta, I served as a chaplain at one of Georgia's state women's prisons. There, behind the concrete block walls of the prison facility, I found myself often asking those questions. Prison is a scary place—it is not meant to be inviting. The barbwire fence seems to reach to the endless sky. My job as a chaplain was not to offer punishment or judgment to the incarcerated women. They had already moved through that phase of our judicial system. My job was to offer care during the time that they were at the prison. My great hope was that I would have moments with a woman in which we together would discover her potential to make better choices. I hoped that she would come to know God's redemptive power and understand that God had been at work, even in the events that had taken place and resulted in her being in prison. I hoped that the woman would desire to live a different kind of life when she was freed.

No matter our circumstances, our location, we all find ourselves together asking the questions, Where is God? Who is God? What does God look like?

We are not the first to ask these questions, and we will not be the last. We are not alone in asking. In fact, people who seemed to struggle with these very same questions have written some of my favorite psalms. The psalmist's words in Psalm 22 echo these familiar words: "My God, My God, why have you forsaken me? Why are you so far from saving me, so far from the words of my groaning?" We listen to the psalmist in Psalm 44 cry out, "Awake O LORD! Why do you sleep? Rouse yourself! Do not reject us forever. Why do you hide your face and forget our misery and oppression?"

I am thankful for the book of Psalms. I love that the Israelites' experiences are compiled into songs and prayers, and in reading these psalms, I find expressed many of the thoughts and feelings that I have had. I hear the anguish and frustration of people who just like me wondered where God was and asked why God was not helping solve their problems. So when my questions about God come up, I go to the psalms.

The text for today is Psalm 46, and most of us are probably more familiar with this passage of Scripture as the hymn "God Is Our Refuge and Strength" than as a psalm. But Psalm 46 is also a promise, and the promise is this: even in those times when we wonder where God is, God is already there with us. Yet God may be with us in ways that we do not even consider.

In the first verse, the psalmist assures us that God is our refuge and shelter. Who would have thought of God in those terms? But the psalmist offers that image—a wonderful image of the strength of our God. God is indeed there, even when the cosmic or natural forces seem to be against us. God's presence causes wars to cease to the ends of the earth. God raises God's voice and others voices are silenced. And God calls to us: "Be still and know that I am God. Be still, relax, trust, and know that I am indeed God."

A preacher friend of mine tells a story about a morning when she dropped her son off at preschool. It was a Monday, and he was very talkative about what had happened at church the day before. Suddenly, he stopped talking and was quiet for a moment. My friend knew his silence meant trouble. Finally, he spoke up from the back seat: "Mom?" Looking at him through the rearview mirror, she responded, "Yes, David?" And then came his question: "Where is God?"

Oh my, she thought, *how do I answer this one? We will be at the school in just a few minutes.*

So she took a deep breath and said, "Well, God is everywhere." David was quiet again, and she could tell that he was deep in thought. She looked again in the rearview mirror and saw him looking around and decided that he must need more explanation, and she said, "David, I believe that God is everywhere, because God is inside of you, and inside of me." And then she mentioned folks that David loved and talked about God being inside them as well, and finally, she concluded, "God loves you so much that God wants to be with you all the time." Once again, she glanced at David in the back-seat, and you can imagine what his next move would be. He looked around some more and said, "God, are you there?"

Sometimes we forget this promise that we find in Scripture that God will be with us, that God is our refuge and strength. Sometimes, we are like children, and we want to see God on our own terms. We want to be able to say, "Hello God, are you there?"

At some of the most surprising times, when I am really honest with myself and with God, I am reminded that God really is everywhere and that God is with me. That truth was made apparent to me one day when I was working at the prison. I met a young girl. I say young because she was twenty-one years old but had been locked up since the age of thirteen. Her grandmother had been her rock and strength the entire time of her incarceration, but her grandmother was dying. The young girl felt guilty because she could not be there to help care for her grandmother. My new friend told me that she had grown tired of praying because her "prayers won't do any good." I struggled to find the words to say to her, yet somehow the words that came out were, "We pray anyway." And I joined hands with her and prayed for her grandmother and for her. Amazingly, at the end of my prayer, she was somehow more at ease, and I suddenly knew that God had been present with her in that room well before I had arrived.

We tend to forget that in the midst of our trials and tribulations, even in our moments of joy and celebration, God is present with us. But often it takes being still to recognize that God is with us—it takes an effort to see God's beauty among us.

Annie Dillard tells a wonderful story in her book, *Pilgrim at Tinker Creek*, a story that has always been exceptionally meaningful to me. Annie writes that during her sabbatical leave from her job at *Harper's Magazine,* she and her husband went to live on an old farm outside Salem, Virginia. The farm was near the college that she had attended. Her sabbatical proved to be a restorative time in her life, for during these days of rest she learned to see the world all over again and to sense its remarkable wonder. Some days she went to the creek and brought back a quart jar full of water. She poured that water into a vitreous china bowl. She waited an hour and then examined the minute trails that had been made by the invisible water creatures on the bottom of the bowl.

One day, as Annie was walking through an old barn, she turned a corner, looked up, and saw a mockingbird flying high above her. The bird suddenly folded its wings and dove, thirty-two feet per second per second, toward the earth, looking as though it were intent on committing suicide. At the very last moment, the bird raised its wings, and Annie saw the characteristic fluting of white that mockingbirds have on their wings and tails. The bird then simply stepped onto the grass—as if it were stepping off an escalator. Annie was entranced by what she had observed and continued contemplating the sight. Later, she wrote in her journal that the experience had caused her to think about that old conundrum about the tree that falls in the forest. You know, if there is no one to hear it, does a falling tree make a sound? She wondered if she had hadn't come around that building at precisely that moment and seen it, would there have been grace and beauty there? She wrote, "The answer must be, I think, that beauty and grace are performed whether or not we will or sense them. . . . The least we can do is to try to be there."[1]

Seeing beauty required Annie's full attention. It required that she be open enough to see it and still enough to recognize it. Stillness is something we do not like to talk about, and stillness is certainly something we do not like to practice. Maybe being still makes us feel lazy, or maybe stillness makes us feel like we are getting older. Or perhaps we live with stillness that is uncomfortable because it is imposed by someone else. But stillness is necessary for us, and my challenge for you is to live into the stillness.

What do I mean by living into the stillness? I mean be looking for the surprising places that God will show up in still places. Be aware of the moments of grace and beauty that you observe when you slow down. Take advantage of the quiet times when you are more aware and can take notice of the new and creative opportunities around you. Be silent, and in that silence ponder on ways you can bring happiness, joy, and love to another person.

Where is God? Who is God? What does God look like? I believe that God shows up in places where we least expect to see God. God shows up in the hospital room, in the homeless shelter, and in the lonely apartment. God chooses to be revealed to each one of us in different ways. So what does God look like? I do not know for sure. But I know that in taking moments to be still, we just might discover that God looks a little different than what we ever dreamed or imagined.

Note

1. Annie Dillard, *Pilgrim at Tinker Creek* (New York: HarperCollins, 2007) 9.

Chapter Nine

Souvenirs and Sticky Notes: Revisited
(Psalm 106)

LeAnn Gunter Johns
2004 Recipient of the Addie Davis
Award for Excellence in Preaching

On October 13, 2002, I nervously entered into this pulpit and delivered my first sermon at Peachtree Baptist Church. "Souvenirs and Sticky Notes" was the title of the sermon preached that day, and today's Psalm text was the passage we read together. I was excited when I realized that I would be preaching my last sermon as your associate pastor during our "Psalms of Summer" series, for it gave me a chance to revisit my favorite sermon. In the six years I have served here and the numerous sermons I have preached, this particular sermon is one that has stuck with me.

I do not expect you to remember what I said on that day six years ago. In fact, in some ways, I hope that you do not remember. I hope that as I have sat with this text over the years and experienced the Spirit's leading for today's sermon, there will be a new message for all of us.

As I have packed up my office over the last few weeks, I have come across many things that I am taking with me as souvenirs from this place. These are things that I want to remember from this time that we have spent together. Most of my souvenirs from this place are connected to happy memories. Some of the souvenirs, however, that I picked up along the way on this journey are reminders of tough lessons or are memories that we all wish we could say never really happened. Souvenirs are our reminders of the past. They provide a wealth of knowledge. They hold memories for us, both the good and the bad.

Our psalm this morning, Psalm 106, is about remembering. The writer of the psalm seems to be pulling out his or her own souvenirs and looking them over. Forty of the psalm's forty-eight verses look back to a time when Israel relied solely on God, a time before the kings and other rulers. In those days, God was the sole sustainer for the people of Israel. So these forty verses serve as a souvenir of a happy time for the people, a time during which they gave their trust to God.

The language of this psalm is very intimate and makes us think that the psalmist was a part of this time of Israel's history. But most scholars believe that this psalm was written during the post-exilic period when the people of Israel were seeking to rebuild what had been destroyed during their captivity. Most likely, the psalmist taps into the corporate memory of the Israelites, is reminded of what God did for them, and then writes in such a way that it seems as if this writer were present. Souvenirs can do that—make you think that you were there. So perhaps what we can say is that the psalmist is remembering back to the stories of ancestors but is also looking for some hope in both the present and the future, seeking to rebuild while trying to find something familiar with the hope of taking the next step forward.

In those post-exile days, those pre-television and pre-electricity days, the Israelites had little more to do after the sun went down than remember. So they sat around the fire in the darkness of the night and told about their travels. They spun their stories. They remembered, and in the telling of stories, they passed their heritage to one another and also to their children. "Do you remember when?" "Let me tell you about the time . . . ." "You do not remember this, but . . . ." No matter who told the story, there was a common theme, and that theme was: despite the fact that the children of Israel over and over again rejected or forgot God, God was faithful in showing them love and saving them.

As they sat around the fire, perhaps the story we read today was spoken out loud by someone—that story about the golden calf that their ancestors built using their own goods. You remember that one? As the people worshiped the golden calf, they forgot who had been their sustainer throughout all of life. They forgot that God had been there with them all along. The psalmist tells us that if Moses had not reminded God that these people were indeed God's children, God would have destroyed them for their behavior.

But because of Moses' words, God remembered that these were beloved children, the people God had created and cherished, and so once again God delivered them. God was faithful.

Psalm 106 continues listing similar events, times in which the children of Israel were disobedient, times when they wandered away, times when they forgot. The making of the golden calf is just one of the many examples. The psalmist tells us that they often gave in to temptation, describing the jealousy of Moses and the people's participation in human sacrifices and idol worship. The Israelites too often gave no thought to God's existence in their lives. They too often panicked when their immediate needs were not met and decided to take matters into their own hands. They forgot about their sustainer, the One who had faithfully provided for them. They forgot their rescuer, who had delivered them time and time again. They forgot.

Then the psalmist tells us about God's response to the people. Certainly, God was angered by their disobedient behavior. But God, in divine love, continued to show acts of mercy to the people. God remembered that these children were the beloved. They were the children of God, and in the end, we read about God's faithfulness to the people of Israel.

The writer of Psalm 106 does not end the psalm with these memories of the past, but based on those memories, the psalmist offers a plea for God's help in the current situation. The opening to the psalm is a prayer of praise to God for the enduring love that is forever. Then the psalmist makes the plea, "Remember me when you save the people." The psalmist recognizes God as the faithful One and thus returns to what is familiar, to this memory of God who has been always faithful and to a time when the people trusted solely in God.

The psalmist concludes with another plea. This time the psalmist moves from using individual language, "Remember me," to using language that reflects the community. The psalmist asks God to save the people as they seek to give thanks to God's name, and then the psalmist breaks into a song of praise of the God of Israel. These words remind us that we must trust God as individuals and trust God together as a community. God works in each of our lives, and God works in and through our communal life together.

As I have been thinking about the souvenirs that I will take from this place, I have been mindful of what those souvenirs will say to me one day about our time together. Included in my box of souvenirs is my ordination certificate. This document is not yet framed—just in case I made an emergency visit to the jail house, I wanted to have my ordination certificate to pull out to verify my credentials. This unframed certificate reminds me that God's call to ministry does not happen in isolation. I am not alone. I have this community of faith—and other communities of faith—that will join with me in seeking to be part of what God is doing. My ordination certificate also reminds me of the courage of this church—for you have ordained many women ministers. I know from my own experience that as your ordination committees sit with candidates and ask many, many questions, members of those committees do not even consider that gender might be a factor in determining ministerial readiness. While this church is not an anomaly, such unquestionable affirmation for women ministers does not happen in all Baptist churches.

Most of you know that I did not grow up in a church that welcomed women into pastoral ministry. In fact, I had never been to a woman's ordination service before attending seminary. But when I came here, you all provided a rich, loving, and nurturing environment, and I felt as though you had thrown open your arms wide and said to me, "God's church is for you too, LeAnn."

Another souvenir that I take with me is a snapshot, a memory of an important moment in my own spiritual journey. A few months after preaching my first sermon here, I felt the Spirit of God leading me toward a newfound love for the people of Ghana. That year I went on my first mission trip to that West African country and worked with our partner, Coast for Christ Ministries. One day during the trip, I preached in a tiny village church with my brother in ministry, Eddie Enim, at my side, translating. I spoke about the story of the woman who met Jesus at the well. For me, that moment was a glimpse of what the body of Christ should be like: female and male standing together, sharing the word of God. During that trip, I also received a very lovely and oversized Woman's Missionary Union outfit from the Ghana women's group, but my best souvenir from my time in Ghana is that memory of standing next to Eddie. It is a memory that I will carry with me throughout my life and ministry and will always remind me of the unique and beautiful nature of the entire Body of Christ.

As I leave this wonderful place, I know that it is not the building of the Peachtree Baptist Church that will be missed. It is you—all of you. But you have given me these souvenirs to take with me. You send me with memories of the mission and ministries that this church has planted in this community and the roots you have put down here. Those memories will sustain me. You have given me, just as the psalmist gave the Israelites, souvenirs that point me to God's faithfulness. By telling me stories of your past as a congregation and as individuals, you have helped me to see how God has worked in your midst. And you have pushed me to look for God's continued working here among you and God's working in me as we all make a next step into the future. I am thankful for a church that has as its purpose loving all people and seeking to do the will of God together.

So if souvenirs remind us of the past, sticky notes remind us of the future. If you have been in my office during the past six years, you know about my obsession with sticky notes. I have sticky notes posted around the edge of my computer, sticky notes hanging from the side of my desk, sticky notes everywhere. The person taking over my office is bound to find some leftover sticky notes after I am gone. Those little yellow notes help remind me of things that are to come.

As a church, we have so many souvenirs. We have so many seminary students who, like me, walked through these doors to find a welcoming people who embraced them and allowed them to be who God created them to be. We have our Ghanian brothers and sisters who visit from West Africa and share their stories with us and inspire us with a word of what God is doing all around this world. We have a wonderful group of senior adults who know what it is like to have deep roots planted in one another's lives through friendship and love. We have a group of younger adults who recognize that there is something different about the people in this place and their commitment to God, and those younger adults want to be part of this community. We have souvenirs. But what about our sticky notes? What is written on our sticky notes? What do they say to us about our future? What is it that God is leading this congregation to do, to be, and to become? My hope for you, my friends, is that you will continue to remember God's faithfulness in your past, embrace one another, and look for how the Spirit of God is moving in your lives and in the world while welcoming all people into God's family.

When I preached my first sermon here, I closed with a story about Carlyle Marney. I would like to tell you that story one more time. Marney was a great preacher, a great leader among Baptists back in the 1950s and 1960s. A man of eloquent and powerful language, even Marney's best supporters sometimes said that to understand the breadth and depth of his message, a person would have to listen to his sermons four or five times.

Walter Shurden tells of a visit made by Marney to New Orleans Baptist Theological Seminary. The great preacher gave a chapel address that morning, and Shurden recalls,

His address was overlaid with so many historical allusions, so many poetic images, so many profound thoughts wrapped in such mysterious language that we all left talking about how great it was, while not a half dozen of us, including the faculty, really knew what he had said. Immediately after the chapel service, Marney appeared in one of the theology classes to answer questions about his address. The first fellow to his feet was a first-year student who hadn't been at seminary long enough to be "cool" and hide his ignorance like the rest of us. He blurted out: "Dr. Marney, I heard you in chapel a few minutes ago, and frankly I didn't understand a word you said. Can you tell me in simple language what the gospel of Jesus Christ really is?" Marney paused, peered over his glasses, and . . . turned, walked to the chalkboard, picked up a piece of chalk, and after waiting an interminable moment, wrote four words on the board in capitals: GOD IS FOR YOU! And he underlined you.[1]

"GOD IS FOR YOU." Perhaps we should all write those four words on a sticky note for our future. With souvenirs of our shared memories of God's faithfulness in one hand and a sticky note with those four words written on it in the other hand, we have all that we need. Together, souvenirs and sticky notes remind us that we have trusted God, we can trust God, and we must continue to trust God. God is the God of our past, our present, and our future. GOD IS FOR US. GOD IS FOR YOU.

"Souvenirs and Sticky Notes: Revisited" was preached at Peachtree Baptist Church, Atlanta, Georgia, on Sunday, June 22, 2008.

Note

1. Walter B. Shurden, *The Doctrine of the Priesthood of the Believer* (Nashville: Convention Press, 1988) 45.

Chapter Ten

Tough Love
(Isaiah 30:18)

Martha Kearse
2005 Recipient of the Addie Davis
Award for Excellence in Preaching

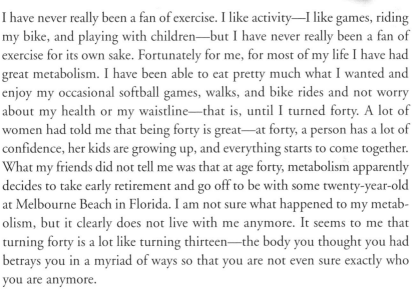

I have never really been a fan of exercise. I like activity—I like games, riding my bike, and playing with children—but I have never really been a fan of exercise for its own sake. Fortunately for me, for most of my life I have had great metabolism. I have been able to eat pretty much what I wanted and enjoy my occasional softball games, walks, and bike rides and not worry about my health or my waistline—that is, until I turned forty. A lot of women had told me that being forty is great—at forty, a person has a lot of confidence, her kids are growing up, and everything starts to come together. What my friends did not tell me was that at age forty, metabolism apparently decides to take early retirement and go off to be with some twenty-year-old at Melbourne Beach in Florida. I am not sure what happened to my metabolism, but it clearly does not live with me anymore. It seems to me that turning forty is a lot like turning thirteen—the body you thought you had betrays you in a myriad of ways so that you are not even sure exactly who you are anymore.

You would think that after a couple of years of sulking, I would have gotten over the shock of losing my metabolism and would have started taking better care of my body. Well, no—not really. I did make some efforts, in a kind of lackadaisical, desultory sort of way. I did some roller blading and rode my bike. I chased my children (and other people's children) and did some swimming. I even tried a triathlon (a beginner's sort of triathlon), which I trained for with my usual attitude of "I don't really need to push it—I'll be fine." In the final race of the triathlon, I crossed the finish line in the middle of the pack, having been passed by several women in their seventies who looked back at me to make sure that I did not need first aid. I also tried some classes at the YMCA, in spite of my dislike of exercise. One time I went with my husband to a Pilates class, which I had heard many people rave about. I did pretty well—faking my way through the stretches and the strength moves—until the teacher told us to get one of the giant red balls. Now, I am pretty sure that Lucille Ball died before Pilates hit America, but if Pilates had been around during the days of her television show, I imagine that she might have an episode about this new exercise craze, and she would have looked pretty much how I looked that day. The instructor told us to lie on our backs and to put our feet on both sides of the ball. Then, we were to press into the ball and pick it up and hold it over our chests. I got my feet on the ball, picked it up, and immediately flung it over my head and into the face of the woman lying behind me. After retrieving the ball, and apologizing profusely, I sat down and waited for the next instruction. The teacher asked us to climb up on top of the ball and balance on our knees. Really? I got one knee up, then, attempting the other, I ended up on my face, spread-eagled, looking not unlike I might be giving birth to a hot-air balloon. Needless to say, I did not return to Pilates class.

As an exercise failure, I wallowed. I made sporadic attempts to get stronger or lose weight or "get in shape," but mostly I wallowed. And I found myself growing weaker—out of breath after climbing one flight of stairs or unable to lift a box that needed moving. But I resisted any attempt to get me involved in a "class" or a program. It never seemed worth the effort. Until a couple of months ago. You know how there can be a perfect storm of attitude and opportunity? I think that is what happened for me. About the same time that I truly became tired of my own behavior (it may have been between Oreo three and Oreo four about 11:30 one night), I heard about a yoga class being taught by a highly valued new friend, Sara. I like yoga. I used to do yoga when I was younger and liked it. So I went to Sara's class. You would think that yoga would be easy since the teachers play that peaceful music and talk so quietly. You might think that right up until the moment when you find yourself with your hands on the floor, elbows bent, head down, and your teacher saying, "Now, if you want, you can put your knees up onto your elbows." If I want? Honesty requires that I answer in the negative on that one. After one such yoga class, I walked around my house for two days hissing like a teapot every time I had to stand up (or sit down or walk).

A few weeks after my first yoga class, another friend, Christine, started talking about a class that she was teaching at the Y called "Total Strength."

I have to say that just the thought of such a class filled me with abject terror. But I like Christine, and she kept encouraging me. So off I went to the Total Strength class. The first session just about did me in. Christine had us using rubber bands and weights, doing lunges and planks, and then doing sit-ups and more planks. The next few days I had to open doors with my lips because my upper arms had ceased to function.

Despite the pain, I have been going back to both yoga and Total Strength. I have missed a few classes along the way, but I keep going. Why? Why would I subject myself to something I do not really want to do? For a couple of reasons. First, I would like for my jeans to fit. Second, I am pretty sure that I am not going to be participating in a healthy regimen of exercise when I am seventy-five if I have not been exercising all along the way. Third, and probably most important, because Sara and Christine have been the face of God for me.

Each of these teachers invited me—they invited me before I had any thought (or desire) to get in shape, to attend a class. Both teachers welcomed me by name when I walked in the door. And both Sara and Christine have, through their actions, said, "I care about you enough to make you do this work—my expertise tells me that you are going to have to push yourself as hard as you ever have to be the strong, healthy person you want to be." Their care for me has been very like what I know of God.

In some ways, God is a lot more like a mother than a father—God's love is the kind of love that is fierce and invasive, the kind of love that always thinks you have some room for improvement. Isaiah 30:18 tells us that God longs to be gracious to us, that God is a God of justice. The rest of Isaiah 30, however, is an excoriation of the people of Israel—a list of their many trespasses and also a promise from God about the consequences of their actions. Remember the context? Despite the fact that God has been utterly faithful in getting the Israelites through scrape after scrape, helping them kill giants, knock down walls, and defeat enemies, the Israelites, in their fear, have gone down to Egypt to get protection (which, based on God's fury at this act, is a little like turning away the protection of your big brother in favor of a gang from the rough side of town).

This passage, most particularly the inclusion of verse 18, makes very clear what justice from God looks like for the people of God—justice is tough love. It is the kind of love that says, "You are going the wrong way— and, since you have been headed the wrong way, going the right way is apt to be painful." In America, we talk about justice all the time. We start talking about it as children, reciting daily the pledge that includes the words "with liberty and justice for all." But we do not talk much about what justice for all requires. We do not teach our children that there is a price for justice, just as there is a price for injustice. We do not have conversations about what justice for all would actually mean. Justice for all would mean that we do not just work in the best interests of the lives of our own children, but instead we work in the best interests of all the children in our community. Justice for all would mean we do not just find a decent home for ourselves, but we work to help everyone have decent housing—even those living in our own backyard, our city. Justice for all would mean that we work tirelessly to make sure that whether or not we agree with each other's philosophies or belief systems, we will protect each other's rights on every single thing. Justice is always standing up, always challenging the status quo, and always letting go of privileges or securities that we think are vital to our survival in order to pave the way for others to have justice. It is never easy, and getting to it is always apt to hurt for a little while.

Isaiah 30:18 says God is a God of justice—and these words come in the midst of a passage in which God makes clear the price of justice. If we dare to question the justice of God, we need only read Matthew 26, in which Jesus begs to be free of the task ahead of him and receives no answer from God. One way to understand that moment of justice is this: in this intimate moment with Jesus, humankind sees as nakedly as ever before in history the cost of injustice. How could there ever be a greater crime than for those in power to bring about the death of this truly innocent man? When humankind controls justice, we get Good Friday; when God controls justice, we get Easter. But there is no Easter without Good Friday, and that is some exquisitely tough love.

Our God is not an easy God. God is not a God of endless nights of watching *Downton Abbey* with a package of Double Stuff Oreos. Like my very fine exercise class teachers, God calls us to dig deeper, to push harder, and to work toward becoming the self that God envisions for us. Our God is the God who allows Gethsemane's silence, who steps back from the betrayal in the garden, who does not intervene at the mockery that is Jesus' trial, the horror that is his flogging, or the grief that is his death. And our God is the God of justice, who out of the darkness of a spring night brings life into an Easter dawn. Amen.

Chapter Eleven

Finding the Horizon
(Isaiah 51)

Shelley Hasty Woodruff
2007 Recipient of the Addie Davis
Award for Excellence in Preaching

My father used to be a pilot, and I remember a piece of information from his flying days that has always stuck with me. A pilot can actually encounter a storm that is so disorienting that he can lose sight of the horizon. The pilot can find herself so completely hemmed in by rain or fog or storm clouds that she loses the ability to see the one most important reference point that should always be right ahead. Losing sight of the horizon is disorienting enough, but when a pilot can no longer see what is ahead, when he can no longer make sense of sky and ground, a curious vertigo occurs during which he can no longer feel, in his gut, up or down. Pilots can be flying completely upside down and have no idea because they are so disoriented. They can be flying straight toward the ground when they believe they are rising toward the sky. There are only two ways to avoid such a situation. The first is to avoid the storm altogether. The second, more practical one is to trust the instruments—to rely on the external gizmos and gadgets that provide information on what is up, what is down, what is behind, and what is ahead.

So imagine with me that the Hebrew people who heard the words of Isaiah 51 were in just such a storm. They found themselves in a terrifying space in which they were so completely inundated by the torrential downpour around them that they could no longer discern up or down. They no longer had a trustworthy sense of past and future.

These Hebrew people were in exile. They had been defeated by Babylon and carted off to an entirely different land. Their beloved temple, where they believed that their precious and powerful God resided, had been desecrated and then reduced to rubble.

The Hebrew people found themselves in Babylon and not in their own land of Judah, facing an uncertain present, not to mention an uncertain future. They were living within a "new normal," one in which they were asked to place one shaky and uncertain foot in front of the other each day and to make a new life for their families when they did not know how to make sense of life. These Hebrews lived with an uncertain existence for so long that an entirely new generation emerged, a generation who only knew the reality of captivity. Their glorious past of living as God's chosen people was reduced to the stories of their elders.

Into this situation, onto this scene, comes the prophet Isaiah. I suppose I should say the poet Isaiah, because chapter 51 is a poem, a thing of beauty. The prophet reaches for words that will restore the Hebrew people's ability to hear—to become aware of something other than the reality right before them. In a sense, Isaiah becomes an instrument that calls the people of Israel out of the disorienting chaos that surrounds them. He speaks into the storm to call them out of it and set their sights back onto the horizon.

"Listen!" he says. "Listen!" "If you pursue righteousness and seek the Lord, please listen to me," he says. Today, too, we listen to the prophet, eager to hear a word that will right us, set us back on track, when we are so disoriented that we cannot feel what is up or down.

See, we are not really that different from the Hebrew people that Isaiah was speaking to 2,500 years ago. Not that different at all. I would venture to say that many of us have over the past few years been given a "new normal" in which to try to live, and this new normal does not quite fit. It is like a coat that is a little too small and a little too scratchy. Not too long ago, we were content to watch the news with our families at 6:00 p.m. in order to understand the world around us. Now we have Fox News and CNN giving news to us twenty-four hours a day, seven days a week, coverage of all that is happening both here and there. New commentators tell us the economy is frightening, the jobless rate is not improving. We all know people who are in—or on the brink of—bankruptcy. Homes in our communities sit vacant in foreclosure. We are constantly being told that our globe is threatened by ecological forces, hurricanes, tornadoes, tsunamis, and earthquakes, all of which ravage our world. Wars and rebellions seem to break out with increasing frequency. Are you overwhelmed just from this list? I am. But this is the world we live in right now. Not a world of peace, but a world of exile and captivity. Not a world at rest, but a world of fear and turmoil.

Even in our own lives, within our own homes, we face personal struggles that consume our thoughts. We deal with disappointments and failures that are so profound that it is difficult to be aware of any sort of horizon ahead.

It is enough to make any one of us become so inundated by the storms around us that we are deaf to anything else. We become so fixated on our present that we fail to see what has been our past and what will be our future. Not much different from Israel at all.

So Isaiah speaks to us today as well as he did to Israel. "Listen," he says. "Listen, and look back." His language is stunning. "Look to the rock from which you were hewn, look to the quarry from which you were dug." Remember what you came from, he is saying. Imagine the sculptor, with scraped and dusty hands, chipping away at the massive boulder in front of him, shaping the nose to be just so, fashioning the ear to curve in such a way. We at once imagine the precision and beauty of this image and the strength and power of rock. We were fashioned with care out of hard, strong stone.

"Listen," he says. "Listen and look back. After you remember how you were created, and from what you were created, remember Abraham and Sarah who gave birth to you." He calls us to remember not just who we were created to be in God, but who gave us our faith, and let us not forget the miracle referenced here. It was Abraham and Sarah who gave birth to us: a couple who could not give birth, a couple who required a miracle beyond imagining to bring a nation into being.

This call to look back is a simple but powerful thing. It pulls at our gut and begins to right us when we remember who we are and what has formed us as people of faith. We not only remember Abraham and Sarah, those exemplars of the faith from the Old Testament who continue to teach us centuries later, but we also remember our parents, our Sunday school teachers, our pastors, our friends—all those in our community who have given us our faith. As I was preparing for this sermon, I haphazardly grabbed for a bookmark buried somewhere deep within the pages of my Bible, and it was perfectly fitting that I grabbed this one. I have not seen it for years and it emerged just now. The bookmark was given to me by Mrs. Leah, my seventh grade Sunday school teacher. I have kept it for eighteen years now because Mrs. Leah was so formative to my faith. I can still remember so much of what she taught me in a time when my faith made sense, when

God felt big enough to cover all of my problems, and when all felt right in the world. When I remember those lessons, I am reminded that in so many ways, all of that is still true.

But looking back to where we came from and what gave birth to our faith is not a call to live in the past. It is so tempting to get lost in nostalgia, isn't it? We look back to a time that we are convinced was better and want nothing more desperately than to recreate that moment. But Isaiah reminds us that when we look back and stay there, we completely lose sight of what God has on the horizon.

See, Isaiah does not let us sit in the present after he asks us to look back. "Listen," he says, and then he immediately pushes our imagination forward to what is next. Armed with the comfort of the past, reminded of how our God is mindful and caring and strong and powerful, let us continue to lift our gaze out of now and look towards what is next.

Listen. The Lord will comfort Zion. Your deserts will be gardens, your wilderness like Eden. You will sing songs of joy and thanksgiving. God's justice will be a light to all the peoples. Listen, for your entire world will be transformed to something more amazing and miraculous than you could imagine.

When the storm is so great that you cannot discern what is up or down, right or left, these words may perhaps sound foolish. Let us not be mistaken here. This is not an easy answer or fix. When we cannot sense what is the way ahead, it takes a great deal of courage and much abandonment of pride to trust something that feels so foreign and counterintuitive, to put every ounce of your faith in something outside of your body, that you have no control over. Listening to the prophet, looking back to who created you, and then drawing from that the strength to hope for a future of comfort and thanksgiving does not feel natural.

My dear friend since elementary school was diagnosed with breast cancer at the age of twenty-nine, and on the one-year anniversary of her diagnosis, as she was celebrating coming through chemo and surgeries and radiation, she was given the news that her cancer had returned. She told me that at first, when the news was fresh and sharp, she gave up. She explained to me that she simply could not see a way out. But when we spoke, she sounded so resolved and strong. I asked her what had changed her mind. She told me, "Well, my doctor came up with a plan. So there is now something to do and try. I came through all of this already, so I know it can be done. I have to hope. I have no choice." I dare say that she still did not *feel* hopeful. But she had looked back, gathered strength from where she could, and decided to put her trust in something completely outside of herself—in God, in her doctors, in her friends and family to sustain her—and she choose to hope. She found the horizon again, a horizon upon which to fix her eyes.

This process is not easy. It is not simple. It does not come without pain or without protest. But Isaiah still calls to us to listen to his words—to look back—and to hope for tomorrow, because that is exactly what we need to discover again what is up or down in the middle of a storm. We know, from the rest of Scripture, that the Hebrew people were rescued from exile shortly after this passage was first heard. They were allowed to return to their promised land and rebuild their temple.

"Listen," says the prophet. "The storm still rages on but, you can trust in what is truly behind and before, above and below." So the prophet leaves us with these words:

Lift up your eyes to the heavens,
and look at the earth beneath . . .
but my salvation will be forever,
and my deliverance will never be ended. Amen.

Chapter Twelve

Can These Bones Live?

(Ezekiel 37:1-14)

Bailey Edwards Nelson

*2008 Recipient of the Addie Davis
Award for Excellence in Preaching*

Many of us have gazed over a "valley of dry bones." We look out and see relationships, communities, and groups torn asunder and falling apart. We know of families, maybe our own, that have been shattered by betrayal, anger, addiction, and abuse. We belong to churches that have divided over theology or worship style or ministry goals. We live in a country separated by partisan politics, by rhetoric, and by the stubborn refusal to even hear the other side and to try to work together for a common good. Sometimes we consider all these shattered relationships, these crushed dreams and hopes, and we assume that they are the end of the story. But perhaps there is more.

When the promising young Hebrews were dragged into exile in Babylon, they certainly understood the realities of death and destruction and hopelessness. They were not where they wanted to be, nor where they were supposed to be. The pain of their past haunted them. Like many of us, who often quit attending church when the times get tough, the Hebrews had a hard time worshiping in exile because they never got over the destruction of their holy city and their temple. They lived with a sadness that permeated all the way to their bones, and they refused to "sing the LORD's song in a foreign land." In many ways, they felt like they had reached the end of the story.

Eventually, the Hebrews were allowed, even encouraged, to return to Jerusalem, but many of them had no interest in returning. For them, the old dream of living in the Lord's presence had died.

In Ezekiel 37, we read of God's presentation to the prophet Ezekiel of a kind of riddle: "Mortal, can these bones live?" Surveying the valley filled with dried, brittle bones, the prophet meekly responds with an exasperated, "O Lord GOD, only *You* know." Pause with me here, for there is an important lesson. Ezekiel's resignation was evident on his face and in the hesitation and depression in his voice. We need to pause to consider his desperation, his hopelessness. If we do not comprehend Ezekiel's struggle here, there is no way for us to comprehend fully the magnificent hope that unfolds in the next verses.

Before we can read ahead and watch the wind swirl the bones back together and marvel at the newly formed humans breathing the breath of life again, we have to stop and ask a few questions. What has brought Ezekiel to the point of near speechlessness and despair? What has caused his community to be so focused on a vision of death? And why the valley full of bones? Why is God so insistent that Ezekiel take a good, long look?

Many of us have not read the backstory in Ezekiel. We do not know what leads up to this grand scene, and so we may not know the answers to those questions. We forget that Ezekiel himself was taken into exile, that he heard reports of his religious institution being corrupted without the proper oversight of the priesthood, and that his status had been reduced from a prominent position as a future priest in Jerusalem to that of a temple-less priest in exile. We forget that his wife has died and that God has commanded him not to mourn for her in order to provide a model for the exilic community that has lost their temple (Ezek 24:16-24). More important, we forget the historical trauma that accompanied this exile. We forget that the Babylonians tortured the inhabitants of Jerusalem; we forget about the siege warfare that lasted almost two years; we forget about the resulting famine, disease, and despair. We forget that the Babylonians destroyed the city of Jerusalem, razed the temple to the ground, killed many inhabitants, and forced the rest to migrate to Babylon. Over and over again, in the chapters we tend not to read in this book of Ezekiel, the prophet describes the multiple traumas endured by his community as they lived with the realities of ancient Near Eastern warfare.

Thus, while Ezekiel 37 is a beautiful passage, it is also horrifying. Chapter 37 calls us to remember, confront, and testify to the devastating events that led the valley to be filled with dry bones in the first place, and that is what God wanted Ezekiel to see, to remember, and to prophesy about. Only within this context of exile and fear of the unknown future can we truly understand the famous vision of the valley of dry bones.

In verse 4, Ezekiel says that the "hand of the LORD" picked him up and placed him in a valley of bones. Then God commands Ezekiel to prophesy to the bones and to tell them to "hear the word of the LORD." In response, the prophet first restores the flesh and muscle, but there is no breath (Hebrew, *ruach*) in them. God then directs Ezekiel to prophesy to the breath and to command it to enter the bones so that they may live. The breath obeys; the bones live and stand together as a "vast multitude."

Following these demonstrations of God's power, God explains to Ezekiel the meaning of his actions: the bones are the exiled house of Israel, cut off and dried up, with no breath or life. But God's word as told through Ezekiel's actions is that the bones shall live, and everyone will know that the LORD has acted. The restoration of the bones stands in contrast to the defeat and despair felt by the people of Israel. This acted parable is repeated twice in verses 12 through 14, assuring the people that Israel will be restored from the "grave" and that they will know "I am the LORD" and that "I, the LORD, have spoken and will act."

The prophetic vision is one of restoration, recreation, and maybe even reconciliation. Ezekiel's vision is not one that is regulated strictly to some distant time past, but rather it speaks to people of all times and places who have encountered spiritual and emotional exile and death. His vision assures the people of his day and the people of our day that restoration is possible, but he also reminds us that true restoration will only occur when the spirit of God moves and is put within the communities and circumstances that need it. The true miracle of this vision is that it occurs after the community has faced such devastating loss.

Perhaps we too often grasp at the promise of new life on individual and communal levels, and we do not take seriously the situations and circumstances that have led to the initial death. We celebrate victory over death, but we refuse to evaluate the systems, patterns, and consequences of our walk through the valley. Fortunately, God's work does not stop when humans have done our worst. God brings to us modern-day Ezekiels. Today, we might see Ezekiel, a young prophet yanked up by the hand of the Lord and slapped down in a small town—where the businesses are dried up and people's hearts are brittle. Ezekiel might walk down the streets in certain neighborhoods, looking at foreclosure properties, seeing those houses without people. This modern-day Ezekiel might be placed in a community wrecked by drugs and violence—a neighborhood in which churches appear to be much like Israel's destroyed temple. They are closed down. Their windows are boarded up. They have For Sale signs in their front yards.

Faced with places and problems like these, our modern-day Ezekiel might find it hard to believe that God could in any way make a difference, and our prophet might respond just as meekly: "LORD God, only you can tell [if these bones can live]."

So what about us? What do we see when we are dropped down in the valley and gaze over the brittle and dried up remnants of our lives? What do we see when we stand and look out at the dry and broken bones of our churches? Should we just give up? Should we give in to the hopelessness, the scapegoating, the fear mongering, the blame game, the greedy grasping for ME and MINE, the violent acting out that seems to characterize our society? Is this how we should deal with the serious issues that confront us? Or perhaps God is calling us, much like God called Ezekiel, and saying to us, "Prophesy to those bones!" They are dry, brittle, and dead-looking. They may, in fact, be dead. But do we believe that the bones are dead, past the point of God's healing, God's restoration? That is what matters. Do we believe that the bones are worthless, hopeless, useless bones incapable of supporting and holding us up anymore?

If our answer is yes, then we should walk away. Just step over the femurs, vertebrae, tibias, and patellas. Listen to them crunching beneath our feet. Walk away. But do not walk away claiming to believe, claiming that God is good and faithful, claiming that the Spirit of the Almighty is present and pulsating among us. Because if we walk away, that is a claim we cannot make.

But if we want to claim the name Christian, if we want to be called children of God, then we must speak with the loudest thunder to those brittle bones. Our voices must rattle with the power of Almighty God, calling those bones to come back to life, back to the purpose for which they were made. If we are the body of Christ, then we must tell that body to get up out of the grave and walk, talk, move, and make life once again.

If we want to claim that, there is one other thing we must do. We must be prepared for failure. Yes, failure. We must be prepared to prophesy to those bones and see no result. We must know that those bones just might continue to lay lifeless before us, and eventually, we will realize that it is not our voice, not our will, and not our power that is needed to make them stand. In that moment, we must remember—just as Ezekiel remembered, just as the people of Israel remembered—we must painfully recall each and every word and deed that led us to this valley of dead bones. We must remember the fights and fears that led to this death. We cannot ignore or forget what brought us to the valley. To do that is to ensure that we will find ourselves standing here again and again.

Instead, we must rattle those bones with a prophecy and power that comes only from God. Because it is, and only is, the power and will and movement of God that can empower us enough to change our situation. It is, and only is, the power and will and movement of God that can bring those bones to life. And for God to work, we must get out of the way. We must blow out the breath that fills our body, the breath that we used to speak words of hurt and pain against other people, the breath that powered us to act harshly against our brothers and sisters, the breath that allowed us to endure trauma and loss and grief, and instead we must breathe in God. Breathe in the Spirit. Fill our lungs with God's Spirit, and that same Spirit will pour forth from us into the bones, and those bones will rattle and rock as muscle comes over them. Flesh will soon cover those bones, and before we can blink our eyes, those bones will be resurrected.

Resurrection: now there is something we as Christians should understand. Each year we sing of the resurrection. We stand beside an empty tomb and gaze heavenward as Christ ascends and kisses us good-bye. We remember that it is the *ruach* of God, the windy presence of God, that keeps us company. We are resurrection people.

If we claim that, if we claim the resurrection, we must breathe it in now. Now is the time. Now is the time to take a long, hard look at the bones of our lives, the bones of our families, the bones of our churches. Now is the time to consider God's question—"Can these bones live?"

Well, can they?

Chapter Thirteen

The Apple and the Tree

(Mark 2:20-35; Genesis 3:1-10)

Nicole Finkelstein-Blair

2001 Recipient of the Addie Davis Award for Excellence in Preaching

Four children, each uniquely gifted, all somewhat oddball-ish, strangers to one another, and each virtually alone in the world, all looking for an escape from their lonely situations. Four children answer an unusual classified ad and become secret agents for the uniquely gifted, somewhat oddball-ish Mr. Benedict, who has learned that subliminal messages are being transmitted from an elite school, the Learning Institute for the Very Enlightened—or L.I.V.E. (which backwards, of course, spells E.V.I.L.). Benedict's receivers have picked up the mind-controlling, double-speaking messages that are voiced by children, but the authorities refuse to believe his claims. As the messages grow stronger, Benedict feels he can wait no longer, so he brings together four children who have been orphaned, abandoned, or run away. They will become students at the institute and try to undermine the evil work from the inside.

In *The Mysterious Benedict Society* by Trenton Lee Stewart,[1] the four young heroes—Reynie, Sticky, Kate, and Constance—are planted in the L.I.V.E. school at its secluded location on Nomansan Island. Hear that? They are embedded at "no man's an island," where they begin to realize that in fact everyone at the institute is alone in the world, just like they are. Every child student and every adult worker is orphaned, abandoned, a runaway, or the victim of a kidnapping. Eventually, it becomes clear that many on the island have had their memories erased, so that every sense of connection is brushed away and replaced by emptiness and prevailing sorrow. Everyone at the institute is an "island"—except, as it turns out, our four friends. For Reynie has come to see himself not as an isolated orphan but as part of a team, even part of a family. "Is this what family is like?" he wonders. "The feeling that everyone's connected, that with one piece missing the whole thing's broken?" Reynie holds tightly to a conversation that he had with Mr. Benedict, whose words seemed like life-saving medicine. Benedict had told him, "You must remember, family is often born of blood, but it doesn't depend on blood. Nor is it exclusive of friendship. Family members can be your best friends, you know. And best friends, whether or not they are related to you, can be your family."

When I read this story the other night, the little sermonizing voice in my head said, "That'll preach!" And actually, it did preach—for very similar words came from Jesus' own lips and were recorded in Mark's Gospel.

Jesus had been out and about in Galilee, calling disciples, making culture-clashing pronouncements about fasting and observing the Sabbath, healing, teaching, and causing unclean spirits to fall at his feet. He had appointed his twelve closest companions, calling them by name. Then the Gospel tells us that Jesus headed home. Mark reports that the same thing happened that always seemed to happen when Jesus came around: a crowd gathered. Some disciples were chosen; but others simply came. That day some simply came; they were a pressing throng, so anxious to get close to Jesus, to receive his healing, and to hear his teachings that traditional hospitality became impossible. There was no room for Jesus and the twelve to rest and eat after their journey. The local religious leaders got nervous about Jesus' obvious power, and they squeezed into the crowd and began making accusations against Jesus. Between the followers and the accusers, it was a full house that day—all those hopeful listeners waiting for a word, all those scribes and religious authorities hoping that the mud they were slinging would stick, and somewhere back there—far in the back of the crowd, barely able to see or hear him—Jesus' own family.

In my family, we have a favorite saying. My mom is usually the one who invokes it, and it can be either a compliment or a gentle insult, depending on the situation—which makes it especially handy! It's an oldie but a goodie: "The apple don't fall far from the tree." (And yes, the bad grammar is intentional! It seems to lose something when you say "The apple doesn't fall . . . .") No, the apple don't fall far from the tree when I would rather work at the sewing machine than get a manicure—that's just like Grandma.

The apple don't fall far from the tree when my dad and brother start talking business; their minds work like calculators and sometimes even a bit like card sharks! The apple don't fall far from the tree when my seven-year-old starts making lists . . . usually I'm making one right next to him!

For every apple that falls close by, though, it seems every family tree also has members who have dropped from the tree, rolled down the hill, over the riverbank, and caught a current that carried them far into the distance. They seem to have forgotten where they came from. They have abandoned their roots. I am sure you can think of a few of these "apples" in your own family; I know I have a few in mine.

I wonder what Jesus' family thought about their "apple." If you look at our Gospel text in different translations of the Bible, you may find a discrepancy. Some translations say "his family went out to restrain him because they thought he had gone out of his mind," while others say "his family went out to restrain him because they heard other people saying he had lost his mind." The Greek is ambiguous—Jesus' family may have been trying to protect him from detractors, or they may have been seeking to protect their own sense of pride. Either way, though, they missed his message. They distanced themselves from him just as surely as did the religious elite who claimed he was possessed. The metaphor is intentional and clear: Jesus is inside—with his followers, listeners, apostles—while his misunderstanding family are stuck outside.

In that overcrowded house, Jesus was physically so far removed from his mother and brothers that he couldn't even communicate with them directly. Their exchange was mediated by the crowd that blocked the way between them. Their messages were passed along like a game of "telephone." But more important, Jesus was emotionally and spiritually so far removed from them that when he looked around for his mother and his brothers, he could not see them at all. Even in that culture where family connection brought security and even survival, Jesus found his family not in those who shared his bloodline but in those who leaned toward him expectantly, ready to seek God through him.

Our other text today is a very familiar story from the Old Testament, a story from the beginning, a story of that first family. Did you ever notice how much Adam and Eve are like us? We often hear the story—the garden, the tree, the crafty serpent, the fruit, the shame—as an explanation of the origin of sin. We can point our finger to this story, and, like a quarreling sibling, say, "They started it! It's their fault!" I wonder, though, if instead of being the original "bad seeds," Adam and Eve are descriptions of all of us, flesh-and-bone children of God who are fully human and who want to be like God. They were tempted not by a piece of fruit but by their own desire to be better, to be more—to have open eyes, to gain knowledge, to be creators and not mere creations. Instead of seeking God's will, they looked around and saw Someone they wanted to be like, and in their desire for like-God-ness, the gave up their true calling: obedience.

The apple, I am afraid, don't fall far from the tree. This is our human heritage—a predisposition to be attracted to the promises of power, to take the easy route to wisdom, to let the world's cleverness convince us that with just one juicy bite, we too could easily be gods.

Back in that packed house in the Gospel of Mark with the crowds surrounding him, pressing close and closer to hear his words, Jesus tries to straighten out our human, Edenic confusion. He preaches that the most important and intimate expression of humanity, the family, is not about being liked, or being wise, but about being obedient. He knows true family does not depend on our shared bloodline but on our shared commitment to doing God's will. He knows that best friends—all those who seek God together, whether or not they are related to you—can be your family.

The English priest and poet John Donne wrote the famous lines,

No man is an island
Entire of itself.
Each is a piece of the continent
A part of the main.[2]

It seems to me that if ever any man could have been an island, it was Jesus. He walked and breathed and lived just as we do. He had every feeling, every temptation, and every experience we have. He knew what it meant to be human. And he was both fully human and fully divine—a paradox, perhaps, but to be sure a uniqueness. In the scope of history, we believe that he was the One, the Only Begotten of God. Surely he of all people had a reason to think of himself as an island, set apart, inherently different, and unapproachably distant. He could easily have succumbed to loneliness and isolation at best, cynicism and narcissism at worst. He could have been singing along with Paul Simon: "I am a rock, I am an island."[3]

But just as God walking in the garden did not want to be alone, neither did Jesus. This Jesus is no island. He welcomed children into his lap, reached out to touch untouchables, healed the sick even on the Sabbath, and sat around tables with his friends. This Jesus did not complain when the crowds surrounded him, disrupted his mealtime, and got between him and his blood relatives. Jesus did not need to build a bridge to connect his shoreline to theirs. Instead, he located himself right there with the crowds, in arm's reach. He was no island, but rather he was a piece of the continent with them; he was a part of the main. And when he looked around at them, he found not just friends or followers, but family.

Hear now the good news: The apple don't fall far from the tree! Right alongside the human nature of Adam and Eve, we have the spiritual heritage of Jesus Christ. He looks around at us, and we become part of his family of faith. Like an orchard of apples, our family of faith surrounds, roots us, raises us up in a love of the truth, and reminds us that we are beloved, known, and never alone. We are invited to come in from the outside, to be near, to listen, to be healed, to seek God and God's will together.

The original hearers of Mark's Gospel found Jesus' words to be encouraging. Scholars tell us that the early Christian community was a group of adult converts to Jesus' way, and most likely there were some among them whose faith in Christ had caused tension and even separation from their blood families. Jesus' words are an encouragement to hearers today whose decision to follow Jesus has isolated them, who may feel distant from their families and their traditions just by virtue of joining in worship on a Sunday morning. Jesus' words are an encouragement to those of us who live geographically distant from our families, as we look for intimacy and try to avoid the isolation of island-hood. Jesus' words are an encouragement to all those who have been biologically or spiritually orphaned or abandoned, to those who have run or walked away from painful past relationships and hurtful church homes, and to those who have felt ashamed in the garden or alone in the world. Jesus' words are an encouragement to all of us. We look around this crowded house, at those hovering closest to us, who alongside us are leaning in toward Jesus, yearning—as we are—to touch his hand and hear his voice. In faith they have become his family, and in faith they are ours as well. Look around and see—just as Jesus saw in the expectant faces of his hearers—see parents and grandparents, siblings and children, aunts and uncles and cousins. In the community of faith, see not just a church but also a nourishing, fruitful family tree.

This is our prayer today:

God,
We are your children.
You know each one of us, and in our uniqueness you name us;

then you call us together and shape us into family.
You raise us up in the way we should go.
You ask us to grow up and to grow together.
You bring mothers and fathers,
brothers and sisters to walk your way alongside us.
Although this life together may not be easy,
teach us to be true companions,
seeking your kingdom, living your desires,
being your body.
As we turn a new page in our family story,
open our hearts to welcome all who are called
and all who simply come,
just as you have welcomed us.
Thank you
for making room for us all
inside your house.
Amen.

"The Apple and the Tree" was preached at Woodland Baptist Church, San Antonio, Texas, on Sunday, June 10, 2012.

Notes

1. Trenton Lee Stewart, *The Mysterious Benedict Society* (New York: Little, Brown, 2007).
2. John Donne, *Devotions Upon Emergent Occasions*, Meditation XVII, 1624.
3. Paul Simon, "I Am a Rock," 1965.

Chapter Fourteen

Stay Loyal to Your Healing
(Mark 10:46-52)

Kyndall Rae Rothaus
2011 Recipient of the Addie Davis
Award for Excellence in Preaching

I am struck by his stubborn persistence. The way Bartimaeus refuses to be silenced. Is it guts, or desperation, or some of both? Bartimaeus jumps to his feet and leaves his cloak behind. If I were blind, I would never leave my possessions behind, for fear I would not be able to find them again. Bartimaeus walks (runs?) to Jesus when he is called. A whole crowd of people, and the blind guy knows without hesitation which one to walk up to. And then Bartimaeus gets what he asked for, but instead of running off to live his life, he *keeps following* Jesus.

I am struck by the crowd's sudden change of tune. One minute they are rebuking Bartimaeus. The next they are cheering him on. Presumably they had been following Jesus along the road, listening intently to the Rabbi's words, soaking up his wisdom. With so many people and so many footsteps, they were straining their ears to hear. And then, this *invasion*: they smelled him before they heard him, and they heard him before they saw him. This dirty unwashed beggar interrupting not just the silence but also the cleanness and the sacredness of the moment, intruding on the quiet anticipation with which everyone else was clinging to Jesus' words. Like the fly that will not quit buzzing or the workmen down the street who will not quit hammering, there is this persistent shouting that is ruining the peace, and the people are understandably irritable and intent on stopping the noise. But to the credit of the crowd, as soon as they see Jesus stop and call the man, they take their cues and change their attitude. They suddenly see the blind man for the underdog he is, and they become instant fans. "Courage! Take heart! Cheer up!" They egg him on to victory.

I am struck by the fact that, although he stops, Jesus makes a blind man walk to him. I mean, it just does not seem very "Jesus-y" to me, to stand there like it's a game of Marco Polo, when it is no game at all to the man who is crying for mercy. Why doesn't God always rush to our side when we are in need? Why must we stand up and walk when we are the ones who can't see where God is, when God knows right where we are?

I am struck that Bartimaeus *re*gains his sight, which means at one time he had it, and then he lost it. How does one lose one's sight? Is it aging, or tragedy, reading without light, or staring into the sun? When did *you* begin to lose the sight you once had? Was it age or tragedy or too much darkness or strain or stress or a general loss of wonderment? When did you stop seeing the beauty of the world, or when did you stop seeing its ripped-apartness? When did things grow so dim that your eyelids drooped as if in slumber? Richard Rohr says that "true seeing is the heart of spirituality today," but "most of us have to be taught how to see."[1] This leads me to wonder, was it Bartimaeus who gained his sight that day, or was it the crowd? Who learned the most about proper seeing?

I am struck that the crowd first saw a filthy beggar, but they kept one eye on Jesus. When they saw him stop and turn, they turned to the beggar again and saw instead a champion of faith who deserved their applause. They began to will him to his healing—was it his faith or theirs that healed him? Maybe it was all the faith mingling together that made a miracle possible.

I am struck that Jesus had enough patience to let all this unfold. Compassionate man that he was, he must have been dying to run over and wrap this man in his arms. He must have felt the urge to scorn the crowd for their initial rebukes and prove them wrong by his show of love. Instead, the text says he stood still. "Call him," he said to the crowd, giving them a chance to change their tone, a chance to participate in the miracle, a chance to cheer on a stranger as he reached for his healing. Jesus could have rushed forward in compassion and rushed the crowd right out of the moment. He could have forced them to be outsiders to the event, and if he were a less forgiving man, he would have been certain that the outside was where they belonged. Instead he offers an invitation to let them be the inviters to a man in need of mercy.

I am struck that though he is blind, that does not stop this man from groping his way to his healing. Healing always feels like groping, does it not? Like you are grasping for straws, like you are following a mirage, like you are teetering on a ledge, like there are not any handles, like you will fall any second and be more scarred than ever, like you might never get there, like you have no idea if the healing is light years away or just around the bend. The movement towards healing always takes place with fuzzy vision and an unclear path, just the soft hint of a voice calling you forward. Sometimes the crowds boo you, silence you, poke fun, and rebuke you. Sometimes you are astounded to hear people cheering you on, believing in you when you do not have enough faith of your own. You cannot control the outcome or the timing. You cannot manipulate things in your favor, and that makes you feel as helpless as a beggar. But your one job is: do not give up. Stay loyal to your healing. Keep asking for what you know you need. Do not let a mob of people shut you down. Because somewhere in that throng is a Savior. Keep on searching until you find your deliverance. Do not be too mad if you are made to get up and walk, because it is the journey that heals you. The journey *is* your faith. We think that faith is an idea in our heads, but faith isn't in our heads. Or we think that faith is something we feel in our hearts, but faith is not in our hearts. Faith is in our legs. Faith is in our bodies. Faith is in how we move, where we go. Faith is the journey we take, and the faithless are those who stay put. Jesus says your faith will heal you.

I am struck that, though the text does not explain this, the crowd must have parted in order to make a path. I mean, they surrounded Jesus, but here was a blind man on the fringes who must get to him. So they cleared out of the way. They did not steer him or push him or force him. They did not point the way to Jesus, because this man could not see them. But they made a clearing, a wide-open space in which he could walk. They did not clutter the way with their opinions. They gave no advice: "Get glasses! Try LASIK! Try religion! Spit and mud are rumored to work!" They said nothing of the sort. They just made Jesus accessible; that is all. They stopped interfering with their rebukes and their wisdom. They parted like the Red Sea and let that man pass through to his Land of Promise.

I am struck that Jesus heals people. I guess it is the pain in the world, or the unanswered prayers, or my own lofty logic that keep me from seeing. Seeing Jesus heal people. It is a *long* journey, but he has healed me too—bit by bit, piece by piece—but I am not so sure that I am *seeing* yet. I am skeptical, cynical, and hard to impress, and I rely on the skepticism to keep me safe from disappointment. But I am starting to learn that I would rather suffer a disappointment or two than never get moving at all. I would rather fall and skin my knee en route to healing than sit on my rump and scorn the difficulties of standing up. I would rather grope my way towards Jesus than keep questioning why he seems to be playing games with me, hiding, standing still. I would just rather *move*, you know? I would rather put one foot in and see whether or not the sea parts than stay put with the assumption that there is no possible way through the chaos. I would rather trust the voices that say, "Come here! Cheer up! Take heart! Courage! On your feet! He is calling you!" than the voices that say, "Shut up! Stay down! You are not worth it!" I would rather be Blind Bartimaeus with a shot at life than the nervous little girl who is too ashamed to beg.

I am struck that, even after you regain your sight, the journey is not over. The first thing you will see is the road. The Jesus way continues, if you follow your eyes. Amen.

"Stay Loyal to Your Healing" was preached at Covenant Baptist Church, San Antonio, Texas, on October 28, 2012.

Note

1. Richard Rohr, *Everything Belongs* (New York: Crossroad Publishing, 1999) 17.

Chapter Fifteen

Mary: A Call to Revolution
(Luke 1:26-38)

Molly Brummett
*2013 Recipient of the Addie Davis
Award for Excellence in Preaching*

We have much to learn from women called by God. For far too long in our history, women have been an afterthought instead of a forethought. Today, Mary will not be an afterthought.

I do have a confession to make. Mary hardly played a role in my Christian upbringing. Perhaps this sermon is an attempt to reclaim her absence in my faith formation. Growing up, I knew Mary was the mother of Jesus. I always wanted to be her in a Christmas pageant, but that was the extent of Mary for me. I sadly think that is the case for many Protestants. Back in the day, some church fathers were agitated by the exalted language that made Mary a co-redeemer of humanity, and in turn, many Protestants, including Baptists, responded by leaving her out of the story, somehow afraid to talk of her calling. Oh, we honored Mary as the mother of Jesus, but we rarely looked to her example. Despite this reality, we could easily argue that no woman has influenced Western history and culture more than Mary. With hope and joy, we should enter her call story, rely on it, lean into it, and allow it to find root within our Protestant selves. So today this Baptist, working for the Methodists, while trying to channel my Catholic brothers and sisters, will attempt to bring some clarity and insight or maybe just share a few ramblings about Mary, the mother of God, and her call to revolution.

Frederick Buechner wrote, "The place Gods call you to is the place where your deep gladness and the world's deep hunger meet."[1] The text in

Luke 1 leads us to ask the question, "Does this calling for Mary meet her at the point of her deepest gladness?" Keep that question in mind.

In Luke 1:26, we meet an unwed girl to whom the angel Gabriel announces, "You will conceive in your womb and bear a son, and you will name him Jesus. He will be great, and will be called the Son of the Most High, and the Lord God will give to him the throne of his ancestor David. He will reign over the house of Jacob forever, and of his kingdom there will be no end" (Luke 1:31-32).

At the time of this announcement, Mary is only thirteen years old, fifteen tops. Her moments of deep gladness should consist of hanging out with her girlfriends by the well or spending time with Joseph as they prepare for their wedding, but then this angel shows up and announces that she is pregnant. How could that news bring deep gladness?

"How can this be?" Mary hesitates and questions her call just as did Moses, Jeremiah, Isaiah, Peter, and countless others before and after her. She wants to know exactly whose idea this pregnancy was and exactly how it would happen. She wants to make sense out of what makes no sense: that God chose her to bear God incarnate. She takes one elongated pause and audibly gives voice to a single question. "How can this be, Gabriel? How in the *world* can I, an unwed, lowly peasant girl, give birth to God incarnate?"

"How can this be?" That is all Mary asked. Unlike Moses, who, after being called, asked numerous questions, paused repeatedly, and then made multiple objections, Mary only took a momentary pause. One moment. If I were Mary, I would have responded like Moses. There certainly are questions I would have raised: Will Joseph stick around? Will my parents still love me? Will my friends stand by me? Will the pregnancy go well? Will the labor be hard? Will there be someone to help me when my time comes? Will I know what to do? You say that the child will be the King of Israel, but what about me? Will I survive his birth? What about me? But Mary does not ask all those questions. She does not behave like Moses. She leans into it. She trusts. She answers the call.

Mary had every reason to run screaming from this angel, every justification for considering him an angel of darkness. Having a child out of wedlock could result in her being stoned for adultery. She could spend the rest of her days in even deeper poverty, struggling to keep herself and her child fed. But she does not reject God's ridiculous plan to inhabit her womb. If I were Mary, I would have felt that this call was not my deepest gladness but was instead my greatest burden. I would have kicked and screamed and told God that God had picked the wrong person for this job. No, thank you. No way am I bearing a child before I have to! Yet, despite reservation, Mary proclaims, "Here am I, the servant of the Lord; let it be with me according to your word."

Mary enters into a call not of her own choosing, yet she does not shrink from the call. She instead enriches all humanity by her willing participation. Mary willingly chooses to enter into the call, enter into the revolution, and enter into the position to help meet the needs of the world. All of creation held its breath, hoping Mary would answer the call. And she does. She gratefully participates in the story.

Mary is not overwhelmed by God's call, but instead lets it flow through her in a song of joy for God's justice. She sings a song that captures her moving response to God's call. Mary had nine months to make sense of her call and what it all meant. Yet it did not take her nine months to make sense of it all. No, Mary's soul "magnified the Lord" moments after hearing and accepting the call. This peasant girl, who did not yet know morning sickness, a swollen body, or the pain of labor, sings praises to God and of God. In the Magnificat, beginning in Luke 1:46, she proclaims,

> My soul glorifies the Lord
> and my spirit rejoices in God my Savior,
> for he has been mindful
> of the humble state of his servant.
> From now on all generations will call me blessed,
> for the Mighty One has done great things for me—
> holy is his name.
> His mercy extends to those who fear him,
> from generation to generation.
> He has performed mighty deeds with his arm;
> he has scattered those who are proud in their inmost thoughts.
> He has brought down rulers from their thrones
> but has lifted up the humble.
> He has filled the hungry with good things
> but has sent the rich away empty.
> He has helped his servant Israel,
> remembering to be merciful
> to Abraham and his descendants forever,
> even as he said to our fathers.

I wonder what her society thought when people heard these words? A revolution is a radical and pervasive change in society and the social structure; a marked change in something; a single turn of its kind. The Magnificat marked such a change. This song of Mary is more than a beautiful anthem that we proclaim at Christmas. It is a revolutionary, prophetic song that gives voice to the call of God for her life and for ours.

Remember the Beatles' auspicious song "Revolution"? "You say you want a revolution, well, you know, we all want to change the world. You tell me that it's evolution, well you know, we all want to change the world."[2] Did the Magnificat ignite the revolution and passion similar to the one experienced in the 1960s in the United States? Did the Magnificat begin a transformation of all people like the Civil Rights Movement did?

In the Magnificat, Mary announced a coming incarnation of God, and her announcement meant the inversion of conventional wisdom. Dethroning political power, plundering the rich, and redistributing food supplies signaled a new age and order. God is about to change the values of life. Her song points to the coming of the greatest revolution that this world has ever and will ever know. Mary's song echoes the Beatles, "You say you want a revolution, well, you know, it's already here."

The Magnificat demonstrates that Mary is a prophet called by God. She hears the voice of God, listens to the call, and speaks to the ways in which God will enter into the broken world. Today, we stand closer to Mary's call than we might want to believe. We exist closer to her response than we might want to imagine. If we identify a prophetic call as hearing God's voice saying that all is not right with the world and responding to that voice by doing something to right the wrongs, then we too are called to be the prophets of our day and age.

Theologian Cynthia Rigby writes that Mary "reveals what it means for us . . . to bear God to the world." What does it mean to say that Mary— and we—are the bearers of God? "It might have been tempting for Mary," Rigby continues, "and it might be for us, to exempt ourselves from the mission to which we are called. 'Sorry, Gabriel,' we might say, 'I'd like to . . . but it's simply not within my power.'"[3] So often we miss out on participating in the grace-full work of God because—unlike Mary—we refuse to acknowledge its impossibility. Instead, we work to make it manageable.

Incarnation is not about manageability. If we are to be the prophets that God calls us to be, we must hear Gabriel saying, "Nothing will be impossible with God," and nod our heads up and down with Mary, saying with her, "Here am I, the servant of the Lord." We with Mary must continue to sing and to live the Magnificat into this day and age.

Like Mary, we are called to be risk-takers, poets, and philosophers. We are called to be agents in God's creativity rather than passive vessels and bystanders. Protestants often dismiss Mary as a passive vessel that bore God rather than the active agent of justice ushering in a revolution. Mary is easier to deal with when she is a flat character rather than the dynamic presence bearing God. Mary's call forces us to realize that we must trust God even when we can't track God. Like Mary, we must sing a song of revolution and dance.

Like Mary, we are called to bear God even when it is socially unacceptable. We are called to bear God in situations that are not always easy, comfortable, or ideal. We are called to face the morning sickness, swollen bodies, and labor pains in order to bring great compassion, love, and hope to places of great sorrow and sadness. We are called to be swollen with compassion like Desmond Tutu, speaking out against the injustice of apartheid; like Mother Teresa taking the last pair of shoes, even though too small, so others could walk comfortably; like Ezell Blair Jr., Franklin McCain, Joseph McNeil, and David Richmond, sitting down at Woolworth's in Greensboro, North Carolina, to protest racial discrimination.

It is not too late too hear the call. It is not too late for your greatest gladness found in the revolution of incarnation and the world's greatest need to meet. It is not too late to respond to the call to bear God into this world. Like Mary, we are called to be storytellers of the revolution. We must tell the world of the radical revolution the incarnation brings. We must show the world how love came down, how it keeps coming down, how with Mary we behold it, and how with Mary we join together and say, "Here we are, willing to bear God into this world and to dance the dance of revolution. Your servants are ready, Lord." Amen.

Notes

1. Frederick Buechner, *Wishful Thinking: A Theological ABC* (New York: Harper & Row, 1973) 95.

2. John Lennon and Paul McCartney, "Revolution."

3. Cynthia L. Rigby, "What Do Presbyterians Believe about Mary: A New Look at Mary," *Presbyterians Today*, April 2004.

Chapter Sixteen

Pregnant Cravings

(Luke 1:39-55)

Brave Journey! Andrea

Andrea Dellinger Jones
2002 Recipient of the Addie Davis Award for Excellence in Preaching

Mary laced up her Nikes and grabbed her overnight bag. She shot a quick text to Joseph. She would not be able to meet for dinner tonight. She was going to catch the next bus to the hill country. If he needed anything, she would be staying with family for her first trimester, and just like that, Mary was gone.

It had been a strange week, to say the least, ever since that angel had shown up. Now Mary was off to see Elizabeth, her older relative. General fatigue, nausea, and headaches were not going to keep Mary at home. The original Greek says Mary left with *spoud*—with haste. She had a craving for kinfolk. There was nothing rational about it. Mary was pregnant.

My last church in Virginia started a ministry for new and expectant mothers like Mary. I was the group's facilitator. At that point, I had never been pregnant or had kids, and I just could not believe the things those moms would do in order to meet together. They showed up at our meeting early, even when they could barely make it on time for church. They would stay late even if they had had a long day at work. They would waddle down steep steps to the room in the basement where we met, even when their ankles were as swollen as grapefruits and their bellies were so big they couldn't see their feet. They would come when they had not slept at all the night before, or when they could not fit into anything except a huge sweat-shirt and sweatpants.

What surprised me the most was their attitude about our meeting in the summer. We began this ministry in the early fall and only took a break for the Christmas holidays. Every other week of the year, we faithfully held our meeting. By the following May, eight mommies had delivered eight healthy babies. I ran over to the hospital at all hours of the day and night for all of those births. So after nine months, I was exhausted. I eagerly suggested that we take the summer off.

You should have seen their pitiful faces when I said that. It was like I had cancelled Christmas or something. One mommy piped up and said she had hoped that we could actually have longer meetings in the summer. At first I thought she was kidding. Then the others starting backing her up. Everyone agreed that they wanted to keep meeting. Majority ruled, and my summer schedule changed.

How dare I stand in their way! Being together invigorated these new mommies. None of them ever articulated for me exactly what that group meant to them, or why the idea of not meeting was so upsetting for them. Certainly, I had noticed their high attendance rate, which was way better than any of the Bible studies our church offered. Yet nobody ever said precisely why they needed this group. Maybe they were just too tired to reflect that deeply. Whatever it was—chemical, social, psychological, spiritual, or a little of everything—I think those same impulses were driving Mary. Her need to be with Elizabeth was anything but rational.

Every year, during Advent, we remember this very pregnant moment. We try to feel some of it ourselves. Over and over again, preachers and Sunday school teachers study this sequence of verses in Luke, all seeking a new slant on this story. How can we feel once again the excitement of a child on its way, and not just any child? How can we get that curious mix of emotions back—hope, anticipation, fear, hunger for deep communion? How can we bypass the intellect and go straight for the gut? Oh, to feel Advent like Mary felt it!

In respectable churches, our effort to recreate this moment is almost comical. Most of the year, we act as if we do not want our emotions manipulated in the interest of piety. But that changes at Christmas! We break out the lights, the wreaths, and the candles! We pull out the fake snow! We deck the stairs with poinsettias! We sing all the good songs! We drag a fifteen-foot-tall evergreen indoors! All those activities make us feel like we have not felt in a year or more. At Christmas, even sophisticated believers crave an entirely different experience. We want a revival of *feeling*, something that is anything but rational.

And that is partly the point.

In the medieval period, all the topsy-turvy festivals came at Christmas. It was the season of reversals, a chance to lampoon worldly powers and structures and systems. It was a time to be nonsensical. On December 6, at the Feast of St. Nicholas, some parishes in England elected a young boy bishop for the whole Christmas season. Even the religious authorities joined in the event. They picked a child from the monastery school or cathedral choir. They dressed him up like the pope and put all his friends in priestly garments. Then these kids processed through the parish, and the boy bishop would bless all the people.

Sometimes this season got even crazier. The Feast of Fools also came at Christmastime. During this annual event, at a number of places in Europe, the laity would don clerical robes and vestments, but they wore them inside out. They burned foul incense. They participated in mock processions and danced in the streets. They elected a mock bishop, who put on glasses with orange peels for lenses. He held books upside down and pretended to read them. The Feast of Fools turned reason on its head.

Of course, the authorities pretty much shut down these festivals by the fifteenth century. I'm sure their motivations were not entirely unfounded. Like most Christian holidays, the Feast of Fools originated as a pagan festival, and I'm sure it often became a mockery of morality as much as anything else. Then again, sometimes people in power have a very difficult time distinguishing a mockery of morality from a mockery of authority.

But there was a good reason why the Feast of Fools made the leap from a pagan holiday to a Christian celebration in the first place. This festival incarnated all the irrationality of young Mary and her *Magnificat*—the prophetic prayer that she offered the day she ran off to Elizabeth's house. In her prayer, Mary says those who fear God get mercy. She says God has scattered the proud. She says God has brought down the powerful from their thrones, lifted up the lowly, and sent the rich away empty. We have to translate this in the past tense, because English does not have the tense that Mary is using. Mary is praying all these things as if God *has* already done it, as if God *is* doing it, and as if God *will* do it.

The problem is that most of us are way too grounded to really feel the foolishness of this. We are certain that Christ did not really change the world the way Mary hoped he would. We still crown earthly kings, and they still milk us. The rich still get richer and the poor do not. People still get sick. People still get hurt. People still get sad. At Christmas, the sad often get even sadder. Sure, Christianity has had its impact on history, but it has a very mixed record. Some of us cannot shake the notion that what we have experienced does not look much like what we thought we were promised.

Besides, Mary's enthusiasm was probably just chemical. If everyone could cook up the cocktail of hormones pulsing through their veins, then we could all experience the true meaning of Christmas every year. We are not surprised when we near the end of Mary's prayer and find this pregnant girl praising a God who "fills the hungry with good things." Mary stayed with Elizabeth for three full months; she probably ate everything in the house.

So at Christmas we can often do little but crave Mary's madness. We hope attending a party or two will be enough. We may take a few days off. We may sit by the fire a little, and it is nice to smell the pine needles, maybe open some presents. But we will not be surprised if we have to watch another white Christmas turn right back to rain. That just makes much more sense than the Magnificat.

A few days ago, a friend of mine stopped by our townhouse and came inside for a few minutes. She had her three-year-old daughter with her. This little girl is only just now learning the Christmas story. She still has not gotten it all quite figured out. So like a good pastor, I pulled my Advent calendar off the mantle for her. My house is anything but kid-friendly, and this was about the only thing a three-year-old child could enjoy in my living room.

This particular Advent calendar has a picture of a stable sitting on a grassy knoll in the moonlight. Every day of December, you pull out one new character of the Christmas story and put it in the Nativity scene. When my friends visited, we already had donkeys and camels and sheep sitting around. Mary and Joseph were already in the stable, too, as well as a few shepherds and one wise man. Baby Jesus should not appear on the scene until Christmas day, of course. Never mind that the wise men in this strange Advent calendar arrive before baby Jesus does. Disregarding calendar correctness, I went ahead and pulled out all the characters for my preschool friend.

I handed the whole scene to my friend's daughter to play with while her mother and I jabbered away. A few minutes later, I looked down to check on our little learner and see how she was doing. I was impressed. By that point, she had completely rearranged the manger scene. She had pulled all the people *out* of the stable and put all the animals *inside* of it. That makes much more sense, of course. Even a three-year-old knows babies do not belong in barns. It is just not rational. Neither is this whole holiday.

Jesus told us his kingdom was not of this world. I guess that is why we do not always see the kingdom. But he might as well have told us that pigs can fly; they just will not do it if we are watching. Or that a falling tree in the forest will not make any noise unless a person is there to hear it. It is hard to get excited about this illusory kingdom.

Yet there is something about Mary. Even the sane believer still craves her *insane* eagerness, her *irrational* excitement. Surely something really did happen in the first century, something as preposterous as it sounds. Mary was waiting for a kingdom to come, a kingdom that already had come, a kingdom that was coming as she spoke. We too wait. We wait with or without Mary's emotion, believing and hoping that the kingdom is nothing less than recklessly unreasonable. Faith is nothing less than the steady resolve to keep banking on this nonsense.

Mary laced up her Nikes and grabbed her overnight bag. She shot a quick text to Joseph. And just like that, she was gone. When she got where she was going, she told Elizabeth the amazing news. The two shared a wonderful moment that we still remember well. Elizabeth, aging and pregnant, was really too old to have her own child. Mary, a teenage mother, was really too naïve to raise the Son of God. She was also overcome, maybe a little out of her mind. But Elizabeth hugged her anyway, and confirmed what she craved: "Blessed is she who believed."

Chapter Seventeen

An Unusual Kindness
(Luke 8:26-29)

Caroline Lawson Dean
2008 Recipient of the Addie Davis
Award for Outstanding Leadership
in Pastoral Ministry

In Luke 8, we find the disciples "on their toes." They are in an unknown land on the "other side of the tracks," a town populated by Gentiles—Gentiles who raise pigs. For good Jews like the disciples, the experience is unsettling. Good Jews do not eat pigs; pigs are "unclean." Adding to their stress, the second that Jesus' foot hits the ground—in this strange land—he encounters a man possessed by demons.

The disciples probably are thinking, "Of course, this makes sense. No big deal. We meet folks possessed by demons all the time back home. It's cool. We got this." More likely, though, the disciples are terrified. After all, this man is not just possessed by a demon. He is possessed by a "legion." Legion refers to a Roman army of around 6,000 troops, so this man has over 6,000 devils haunting him. Such information could not have been encouraging for the disciples. If I had been one of Jesus' followers, I would have had one foot on the ground and my other foot in the boat ready to head home. Just say the word, Jesus, and I am gone.

This is scary stuff. The possessed man lives in the tombs, is naked, and is bound by chains. The people in town hire a guard to watch over him. Scary stuff indeed. When the disciples see this man in his exposed state and hear him screaming at Jesus, they have to be thinking that they have just walked into a horror story, and as for me, if I think about this encounter too long, my skin starts to crawl, and images from all those scary movies that I watched as a kid pop into my head.

So if I had been in the disciples' shoes, I surely would have sprinted for the boat. But the problem with running away is that there is a great danger of missing a formative moment, missing the lesson. This encounter with a possessed man has the potential to teach us not to equate difference with demons or to equate the unknown with something that will hurt us. If we stay in the moment, we just might realize that the unknown can teach us about faith.

While the disciples and I react with fear and uncertainty to this man in the tombs, Jesus has a different reaction. Jesus sees the man falling at his feet. Jesus hears the man cry out in a loud, booming voice, "Leave me alone." And instead of running away, Jesus has the courage and the kindness to stick around.

Jesus asks the man, "What is your name?" The man answers, "Legion," a heart-wrenching moment in which Jesus realizes that the man has lost his true identity. He only knows himself and names himself by his hurt and pain. He identifies himself, labels himself by this legion of demons that has overtaken him. In our world today, people continue to label themselves according to their suffering. How many people do we know who are defined or who define themselves solely by their suffering "label": alcoholics, schizophrenics, addicts, homeless, illegal immigrants, and terrorists. *We give them one story.* We give them one name. They are defined by their struggle. We ignore the complexity and the beauty in their lives that grants them strength in the struggle. Instead, as individuals and as a society, we define people by the taboo "demons" that push them to the margins. We ignore their humanity. And all too often we flee, running from them in fear.

But Jesus stays. His remaining with Legion may be the most important moment of unusual kindness in this story. Just by staying, Jesus changes the situation. His presence is noticed by the demons and disturbs them so much so that they ask to be cast into this herd of pigs that are on the hillside. The demons fear Jesus, and in another act of kindness, Jesus agrees to send the demons into the pigs. But here is another bizarre scene. The text tells us that the pigs head straight into the lake and drown. Tradition tells us that there were 2,000 pigs overcome by these devils.

On my first trip to Nicaragua with Peaceworks, my group was in a rural area in the mountains. One lovely afternoon, we went shopping for handicrafts, and in the midst of a peaceful day, we heard tortured sounds. Some creature was making high-pitched, otherworldly noises just down the street from us. The poor creature sounded as if it were fighting for its life. We all decided that someone must be killing something. But when we investigated, we discovered that the creature was a pig that had been strapped to the roof of a bus so that its owner could take it to be sold at the market. The pig was not happy. It was making those horrific noises, noises that again made my skin crawl. In that moment, I felt great sorrow for that pig, that loud, scary pig whose unhappiness, I am sure, continued to be heard all the way down the mountain.

One pig made that huge scene. We could hear the squeals all over town. The pig demanded our attention. Now multiply that sound, that experience, times 2,000! I can only imagine 2,000 pigs running down a hill, squealing the whole way, throwing themselves into the water, and violently drowning. That image sticks with me, and I think of this poor man, this man who had been plagued by devils, who had been living with that chaos inside of his head, in his body, in his relationships, in his soul. I sense his intensity, his desperation, and his insane, painful reality, and I do not know what to do with that level of pain. Most of us cannot handle seeing or hearing that kind of pain. We do not know how to be kind to a person like that.

Immediately after the pigs fling themselves into the water, the pig herders show up. They are owners of the pigs, caretakers of the pigs, and they are invested in the well-being of their herd. Yet their arrival only adds to the chaos. They cry and shout. They grieve the loss of their entire source of income, the loss of financial stability that will hurt their family for generations. These pig herders' lives have been turned upside down by the outsider named Jesus.

Because of the chaos, the townspeople run Jesus off. They do not see him as a healer, teacher, or demon exorcist. What if they had? What if they had taken advantage of his power? What if they asked him to come into town, to have dinner? What if they had asked him to take a look at their sick relatives, their hurting friends? After all, this Jesus had just healed Legion, their problem resident, their chief pest, this naked guy who lived in the cemetery. No longer do they have to worry about steering their kids away from the tombs. But instead, they rush to judgment, pushing Jesus out. Why? Why are they in such a hurry? We do not know why. The obvious reason seems to be that they are afraid that Jesus will kill more livestock, that he will financially ruin the entire town. But I also think there is something scary and powerful about this idea that when Jesus comes to town, suddenly demons are being cast out. Demons are flying. Demons are on the loose. The people now must be wondering: are these demons contagious?

Can we trust this Jesus person? If we let him stay, will he attract more crazy people to our town? He just murdered a herd of pigs, sent families into financial ruin. Sure, he healed the crazy guy who lives in the tombs, but what about us? And in the end, they shout, "Leave us alone, Jesus!" The disciples again hope that maybe this time they can "jump ship." Maybe they can leave this strange place behind, and this time they get their wish. Jesus leads them to the boat, and they get in.

But suddenly, the healed man appears at the edge of the boat. This man who was possessed by 6,000 demons is now clothed and in his right mind, and he asks, "Jesus, can I come with you?" But Jesus replies, "Stay, return to your home, and share with everyone how God has healed you." In so many ways, it would be easier for Legion to leave his home country, to move away, to start over. But Jesus says, "Stay." So Legion makes his home at home and has to face the realities of his own community. He has to face those who shunned him and those who will continue to shun him. He has to face those whom he hurt while he was under the influence of the demons. This path—although in many ways it is harder than leaving—promotes his healing, his restoration to his community. On this path, he has to face the challenge of forgiving himself and forgiving others. He has to be vulnerable and ask others to forgive him, and forgiveness is the real secret to exorcising our scariest demons.

The first question that this story asks of me is simply this: Why are we so afraid of mental illness, schizophrenia, depression, bi-polar illness, addiction? Why are we so afraid of those who are institutionalized?

We often root for an underdog in sports settings. But we do not root for the underdogs when it comes to mental illness. Our bias for the underdog only goes so far. We do not cheer for, support, and care about the most taboo people among us, those living on the margins of the margins of society, for they present a risk to us, and when there are threats to our own psychological and physical security, a part of our brain takes over and says, "Stay away from that person." Our brain begs those kinds of people to "Leave us alone."

I also wonder if we are afraid of mental illness and those folks who live on the margins of the margins of society because they remind us of our own demons, our own frailty. They remind us that sometimes suffering and pain are cast upon us, and sometimes we are utterly out of control. Their baggage, their fears, remind us all of our own demons—and that is not a very pleasant reminder. Or perhaps we are afraid on some subconscious level that if we hang out with the frail, the dying, the mentally ill, if we befriend people who are struggling with demons, if we hang out with the ostracized, then their suffering will be cast upon us.

The last question that I will leave you with is simply this: How is Jesus able to tap into a source of unusual compassion when he encounters this tortured soul? What gives Jesus a different perspective? What allows him to tap into such brave kindness?

My theory is that Jesus somehow sees through the legions of demons, the pains, and the baggage that haunts the possessed man, that haunt and possess us. He sees past all the hurts that we collect over a lifetime, and despite our demons, he sees us. He sees our true selves. He knows our real identity. He knows our name.

In the chaos of this story—the pigs squealing, the demons begging, the disciples freaking out inside, the pig herders weeping—Jesus sees this man. He knows this man's true identity. Jesus recognizes this man's humanity. Jesus honors this man's connection to all of us. Jesus sees that this man is beloved by God and that he is created to be beautiful and to be cherished. And in kindness Jesus reaches out and draws the man's true self forth. That is the miracle! How can we love each other like that? How can we love the least of these? How can we be in touch with Jesus' miraculous kindness in our own most unlovable hidden places? How can we be a catalyst for unusual kindness in the world?

Finally, what are the 6,000 devils that plague you? What are the pains and hurts you are living with? For me, this story boils down to something pretty simple: if God's love can cast out a man's legion of 6,000 devils, God can love me in my struggle, and God can love you in your pain. God's love is tough and resilient. God specializes in unusual kindness. When we think we are beyond a miracle and are living in despair, if we move to put our demons at Jesus' feet, we will hear him say, "What is your name?"

Jan Richardson wrote a powerful poem—words for us to ponder:

From the hundred wants
that tug at us.
From the thousand voices
that hound us.
From every fear
that haunts us.
From each confusion
that inhabits us.
From what comes

to divide, to destroy.
From what disturbs
and does not let us rest.
Deliver us, O God,
and draw us into
your relentless
peace.[1]

Note

1. Jan Richardson, "Delivered: A Blessing," *The Painted Prayerbook* (paintedprayer-book.com).

Chapter Eighteen

Troubling the Teacher
(Luke 8:40-56)

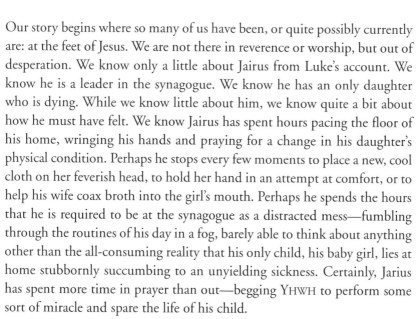

Shelley Hasty Woodruff
2007 Recipient of the Addie Davis
Award for Excellence in Preaching

Our story begins where so many of us have been, or quite possibly currently are: at the feet of Jesus. We are not there in reverence or worship, but out of desperation. We know only a little about Jairus from Luke's account. We know he is a leader in the synagogue. We know he has an only daughter who is dying. While we know little about him, we know quite a bit about how he must have felt. We know Jairus has spent hours pacing the floor of his home, wringing his hands and praying for a change in his daughter's physical condition. Perhaps he stops every few moments to place a new, cool cloth on her feverish head, to hold her hand in an attempt at comfort, or to help his wife coax broth into the girl's mouth. Perhaps he spends the hours that he is required to be at the synagogue as a distracted mess—fumbling through the routines of his day in a fog, barely able to think about anything other than the all-consuming reality that his only child, his baby girl, lies at home stubbornly succumbing to an unyielding sickness. Certainly, Jarius has spent more time in prayer than out—begging YHWH to perform some sort of miracle and spare the life of his child.

We know that prayer. In the early days of our desperation, it is a full, thoughtful argument for God's intervention. We list all the reasons why we have faith that God can perform said miracle, why our situation so very much needs God's care. Perhaps we even barter with God, promising that we will be better people of faith if God would just do something. But several days into our exhausted prayer, we find that it has been reduced from the careful monologue to an almost guttural utterance of, "Please, oh please, oh please . . . ."

It is this version of Jairus who finds himself flinging his abbreviated prayer along with his whole body at the feet of Jesus, begging Jesus to come to his home and do something—anything—to save his baby girl. And while we are not told what Jesus said in response to such a display of broken desperation, we are told that Jesus, and the crowd, began to move in the direction of Jairus's home.

Jairus is perhaps now yards away from his miracle. After an agonizing wait for his one greatest desire to be granted—the health of his daughter—he finally has the attention of Jesus. The great miracle worker who has already cast out demons, vanished fevers, cured leprosy, raised a widow's son, healed a paralytic, and calmed a storm is now—finally—on his way to extend his touch to one precious little girl on the brink of death. The miracle is on its way! Jairus can almost imagine that his daughter's healing could become a reality. His heart has quickened, already altered from its slow, labored beating from having such a great weight placed upon it to a near dance of anticipation. His eyes have widened in amazement. He no doubt trembles from sheer excitement. His miracle *is* coming, the miracle for which he has been begging for who knows how long as he has had to watch his daughter decline.

Jairus leads Jesus, having to strain every muscle in his body not to run ahead, pulling Jesus behind him toward his home. Yet before the miracle arrives for Jairus's daughter, the miracle stops. There is an abrupt halt in Jairus's story as a hemorrhaging woman enters the scene. Jesus stops walking towards the dying daughter and instead tends to the daughter who has just touched the fringe of his clothes. In a quite beautiful moment, Jesus does not dismiss the action and continue to move on. This Jesus demands to know who it was that has just touched him with such deliberation. When the answer does not come immediately, this Jesus waits until he finds it, and then this Jesus listens—for as long as is necessary—to the woman's story. He does not hurry her up, fill in the details, or cut her off. He listens as a grateful, fearful, and emotional woman recounts her twelve-year ordeal and tells of what has occurred in her life.

Meanwhile, Jairus stands—watching, desperate. Time is ticking by with every word that this woman says. Every moment that she recounts the miracle that she has received is another moment that Jairus's miracle lies feverish and dying. What a conflicted, out-of-control feeling. The muscles in his body rejoice in what he has just seen. His miracle worker has just proven himself again, and how wondrous it is that this woman has been so fully restored! Surely the beauty of this is not lost on Jairus, who can see the look of unadulterated joy spread across this woman's face as she looks into the face of Jesus. This is a celebration! At the exact same moment, Jairus stands there watching the scene in panic. His insides are aching with both jealousy and fear as his forward movement has stopped, and he stands—quite out of control of the situation—as his miracle is delayed.

Jesus' attention is still on the woman, when someone comes from Jairus's home and says, "Your daughter is dead. Do not trouble the teacher any longer." The miracle that was so close—perhaps feet from the threshold of Jairus's home—is no longer needed. It is too late. Do not even bother troubling the teacher any longer.

I hope that you have never felt like Jairus must have, but my guess is that more of you have than not. I certainly have. I have begged at the feet of Jesus, babbling pathetic, truncated prayers knowing that my time for a miracle is quickly running out, and I have stood, outwardly celebrating someone else receiving a miracle. I have looked into their jubilant, dancing eyes and smiled as wide as I could, cursing myself for having my joy for them tainted with a sense of increased desperation for my own lack of miracle. I have certainly thought, "It is too late. Do not trouble the teacher anymore."

Trouble. What a word. But it is true. When your sight is so fixed on one goal—one miracle—that will not come, how tempting is it to feel that your ceaseless nagging and begging at the feet of Jesus must just be a bother. Straighten up, you tell yourself. Alter your expectation. Seek help elsewhere. Resign yourself to the fact that your miracle will not come. Stop troubling the teacher.

Thankfully, the story does not end with those words. Jesus is not unaware of what is going on with Jairus simply because he has taken time to look upon someone else. His attention towards one child has not removed it from another. "Do not fear. Only believe, and she will be saved," he says.

It is not logical. It does not make sense. No matter how thoroughly I exegete it or parse it, it just does not compute. At the moment that Jairus's hope for a miracle has vanished, he is told to keep troubling Jesus. Choose belief over fear, for this is not the end of the story. The end of the story is Jesus taking the little girl by the hand, helping her out of her bed, and then asking her family to give her something to eat with Jairus looking on—no doubt stunned and half disbelieving—as his miracle has arrived.

"Do not trouble the teacher anymore." Honestly, that is our natural reaction. After we have desperately thrown ourselves at the feet of Jesus—praying that the cancer might go into remission, that the pregnancy might be sustained, that the child will recover from the brain injury; after we have been teased with the prospect that our miracle might be on its way—when the cancer responds to treatment, or the sonogram shows a heartbeat, or the monitors show signs of brain activity; and after we seem to be put on hold when things turn for the worse while we watch another get their miracle—when the cancer returns while a coworker earns her "survivor status," or the friend gives birth to her first child without worry or complication, or the child down the hallway leaves the hospital for good; after all of this, it is so easy to shrug our shoulders, stop even our two-word prayers, and stop troubling the teacher. If we could only see Jesus turning his attention from those who have received his most recent miracles and hear him say to us, "I have heard you all along. You have not been forgotten. Do not fear, only believe." If we could only realize that our friends coming to tell us the news that all hope is lost is *not* the end of the story. If we could only continue to lead Jesus to our homes, despite every indication that it is silly to do so.

Do not hear me wrong. I am not so Pollyanna-ish to believe that all situations can be overcome with more prayer or belief, or that a miracle will always arrive on this side of the grave. Indeed, sometimes that does happen. Just because things are not occurring within our time line, and our prayers are tired and weary from use, and every indication from what we can see in our finite vision is that Jesus is off elsewhere tending to other individuals, we would all do well to remember that the time to abandon hope and stop troubling the teacher has not come. Yet even in those more heart-wrenching situations where our need for a miracle truly *is* finished—when our friends arrive to inform us that everything is over—Jairus's story reminds us that *our* story is not over with death. Even death is no reason to stop troubling the teacher. This hope—this radical, eschatological hope in a Christ who redeems beyond death and restores people to wholeness on this side of the grave and on the other—is not an empty salve to apply in our deepest pain. It is a defiant claim that death does not have the final word and that our Christ continues to walk with us, hear our prayers, listen to our heart's most desperate needs, and be led across our very thresholds despite the existence of death, despite the appearance that all is over.

Never stop troubling the teacher. When your knees are about the give out as your weight rests upon them at the feet of Jesus, do not stop troubling the teacher. When you stand completely conflicted, watching someone else's miracle in both hope and anguish, half-convinced that Jesus is too busy elsewhere, do not stop troubling the teacher. When you are certain that your need for a miracle is no more, do not stop troubling the teacher. It may make no sense. It may not be logical. It may hurt like nothing you have experienced before. You and your friends who are in the midst of mourning may be tempted to laugh at Jesus telling you otherwise. That is okay. But do remember that Jairus's story does not end in death, and neither does ours. Even death is no reason to stop troubling our Christ, our teacher.

Chapter Nineteen

Instructions for the Journey
(Luke 9:57–10:11, 16)

Heather Mustain
2013 Recipient of the Addie Davis Award for Outstanding Leadership in Pastoral Ministry

As a resident chaplain, I find myself almost daily asking students about their spiritual journey, and, when beneficial, sharing a bit of my own journey with them. There is a multitude of ways in which we ask each other about our relationship with Christ. Instead of asking about a student's spiritual journey, I could ask how their walk with God has been, or I could request that they share about their daily devotional life, or I could inquire as to how God has spoken to them lately during their quiet time. But I like the word "journey," and I use it intentionally.

Some may call it a matter of semantics, but for me the word "journey" has deeper implications that I hope help inform and shape my own communication about God. For me, journey implies that neither they nor I have quite arrived at perfection, and in order for us to journey, we cannot be still. Journeying requires movement.

Journeys tend to lead us to adventure. They are almost always unpredictable. Sometimes we feel up, and sometimes we feel down; sometimes we turn left and other times right. We are never really certain about what awaits us around the corner. When I think of embarking on a journey, I always think of other people because, if I am honest, I do not like journeying alone. Journeys are meant to be communal experiences. Journeys extend an invitation to others to join us in our adventures. Ultimately, the arrival at our destination does not transform us; the journey transforms us. Maybe this is what is meant by those who say, "Life is a journey, not a destination."

Our text in Luke 9 is the beginning of Jesus' long, slow, and steady journey toward Jerusalem. Over half of Luke's Gospel is dedicated to this journey from Galilee to Jerusalem. The turning point of Jesus' ministry in Galilee has been identified as Luke 9:51—the verse that tells us that Jesus set his face to go to Jerusalem, a verse that offers the reader a sense of foreboding of what is to come. Ten chapters later, the reader finally finds Jesus, riding on a donkey, weeping over Jerusalem, entering the city in which he will eventually be put on trial and sentenced to death. This is the final destination for both the readers and Jesus' journey. Scholars have noted that Luke takes his time in reporting on Jesus' journey. Luke believed that something powerful happens when we embark on a journey, and thus, he allows the reader ample opportunities to be transformed. But it is not until we arrive at the destination that we truly understand how the journey has changed us.

Now, I do not think it is coincidental that Jesus' journey begins with rejection. The Samaritans' outright rejection of Jesus only emphasizes the foreboding feeling of the consequences that this journey will have. Immediately following the rejection, Jesus spells out the demands of following him, explaining exactly what the costs of being a disciple on this journey will be.

My husband, Chad, and I are finishing the last of our four years at Truett Seminary. There are a great number of things that we are thankful for as we look back over the years, but there also are a great number of things we look forward to as we begin to dream about our future. One of our dreams is a hope soon to own furniture that did not come in a box. You know, "box furniture." You buy a big box that has a bazillion pieces of "stuff" in it, and somehow, that stuff magically is transformed and suddenly resembles something like a bookshelf. Have you ever tried to put together furniture in a box without using the instructions? It is nearly impossible, unless, like Chad and I, you have owned numerous bookshelves that came out of a box. We have become master bookshelf assemblers. But even as master assemblers, there still comes a point where the instructions are needed because, although the pieces are labeled A through J, A does not necessarily connect with B or B with C. Only by reading the instructions can we walk away (1) still married and (2) with something that resembles a bookshelf.

Instructions matter, and Jesus knew the importance of good instructions. In Luke 10, much like a doctor would give a patient instruction for continued health, Jesus gives the Seventy instructions about how to prepare the cities for his arrival. The sending of messengers in teams of two occurs throughout the book of Luke, and the running ahead to announce Christ's coming not only implies preparation but also gives the mission a magisterial tone. Commentaries attribute Luke's emphasis on the Seventy as foreshadowing the Gentile mission that is found in Luke's second book, Acts. The number seventy seems to coincide with the seventy Gentile nations listed in Genesis 10.

In Luke 10:3, we find the first of Jesus' instructions: "Go on your way. See, I am sending you out like lambs into the midst of wolves." Jesus' words are a fulfillment of Isaiah's prophecy that wolves and lambs will one day dwell together in peace. He then commands the disciples that, upon entering a house, they are to first say, "Peace to this house!" knowing that the reaction of the people to the disciples would function as their response to Jesus himself.

Then comes Jesus' second instruction: "Carry nothing; no purse, no bag, no sandals." His desire was that the Seventy be utterly dependent on strangers. Jesus wanted his followers to work from a position of equality, if not dependency, as they sought to carry out his ministry and message. In *Friendship at the Margins,* Christopher L. Heuertz and Christine D. Pohl write, "When we allow ourselves to be disarmed, we become both vulnerable and strong. We choose the way of Jesus, laying aside all the earthly resources that give us power—in order to be present to those we love."[1] By carrying nothing, the disciples made themselves vulnerable, and in their vulnerability their message became stronger.

If the peace offered by the disciples was accepted, they were instructed to stay a while with their new hosts. In Luke 10:7-8, Jesus tells them, "Remain in the same house, eating and drinking whatever they provide, for the laborer deserves to be paid. Do not move about from house to house. Whenever you enter a town and its people welcome you, eat what is set before you." In those days, according to my seminary professor, Andy Arterbury, offering a stranger hospitality included the host's implicit vow to also provide protection. Yet Jesus' instructions were not directed just to those offering hospitality but were also given to the disciples who were accepting hospitality. Jesus tells them, "Eat what is set before you." In other words, Jesus asks the Seventy not to allow cultural differences to hinder his ministry and message. He says, "Do not move about from house to house." Jesus reminds them to accept what is provided willingly and not to seek more prestigious or luxurious accommodations. Jesus' intentions seem clearly to establish hospitality as a truly interdependent and reciprocal relationship between strangers. For the Seventy and for us, hospitality is powerful, powerful enough to bridge the gaps that existed between people of different regions and cultures. Ultimately, we know that hospitality will become the means through which the Gentiles will be integrated into the life of the church.

In Luke 10:9 and again in Luke 10:11, Jesus repeats an instruction twice. He tells the Seventy to deliver the message that the kingdom of God has come near. For indeed, the kingdom of God has come near to those who accept these Seventy followers of Christ. The kingdom of God also has come near to those who reject them. Acceptance or rejection—the message is the same; it is an invitation to join the journey. There will come a time for judgment, but those judgment decisions are not for the Seventy to give. Their role is simply to invite. If the invitation is refused, they are assured that they are only accountable to God for issuing the invitation. What dominates the instructions of Jesus to the Seventy is that they are to spread a message of ultimate hope and forgiveness.

Scott Cairns has written a series of poems called "Adventures in New Testament Greek" in which he explores the agency of words. His poem, "Hairesis," examines the word "heresy" and also addresses the judgment that has befallen those condemned by the church of heresy. Cairns confronts readers with the agency of his own words:

Historically—which really has to be the toughest
circumstance in which to figure Him—supposition
hasn't always met with sympathy. No,
you don't need me to underscore the poor
reply with which the body has from time
to time addressed its more imaginative
members, but I would admit what shame
we share, allowing pettiness and fear
to acquire the faint patina of a virtue,
butchery, an ecclesiastical excuse.
Does one always *make* one's choices? From what
universal view of utter clarity
might one proceed? Let me know when you have it.
Even heretics love God, and burn
convinced that He will love them too.[2]

After the rejection of the Samaritans in Luke 9, the disciples ask Jesus, "Lord, do you want us to call down fire from heaven to destroy them?" Should we burn them? Jesus turns and rebukes them. His verbal response is not recorded by Luke, but perhaps Jesus replied, "The kingdom of God has come near to them as it has come near to us. God loves heretics, and heretics just might love God too." Like the disciples and the Seventy, we are never instructed to judge; we are called to invite others to the journey, a journey that promotes peace, dependency, and mutual support.

One of my favorite recent reads is John Steinbeck's *The Grapes of Wrath*. The story tells of the Joad family's journey from Oklahoma to the Promise Land (California) in the late 1930s. The Joads have experienced the devastation of agricultural failure. They are caught in modernity's movement towards bigger and better, and eventually, they are forced to pack all their belongings and leave what they have always known. But it is not the Joads' arrival in California that changes the family (or changes the readers). Instead, the transformation comes from what happens along the way. The Joads experience intense suffering, and their journey to the Promise Land is filled with incredible pain and loss. Yet because of the support they receive and their mutual dependency on other travelers, they find hope. Listen to Steinbeck's words about those who participated on this journey: "In the evening a strange thing happened: the twenty families became one family, the children were the children of all. The loss of home became one loss, and the golden time in the West was one dream."[3] Twenty families became one family. Children were the children of all. Losses and dreams were shared.

We have been called to a long, slow, and steady journey. As we continue on this journey, may we be reminded of the instructions Jesus gave to the Seventy. May we be disciples who promote peace, dependency, and mutual support. May we never seek to hand out judgment but to extend invitations—always declaring that the kingdom of God is near.

Notes

1. Christopher L. Huertz and Christine D. Pohl, *Friendship on the Margins: Discovering Mutuality in Service and Mission* (Downers Grove IL: IVP Books, 2010) 97.

2. Scott Cairns, "Adventures in New Testament Greek: Hairesis," in *Compass of Affection: Poems, New and Selected* (Brewster MA: Paraclete Press, 2006).

3. John Steinbeck, *The Grapes of Wrath* (New York: Viking Press, 1939).

Chapter Twenty

Help Wanted: Harvesters for God's Vineyard!
(Luke 10:1-12, 17-20)

Veronice Miles
1999 Recipient of the Addie Davis Award for Excellence in Preaching

In Desmond Tutu's *An African Prayer Book* is a poetic prayer titled "Reflections on Wholeness" that calls us from the busyness of life and challenges us to consider the interconnectedness of the entire human family:

> *Busy normal people:* the world is here.
> Can you hear it wailing, crying, whispering?
> Listen: the world is here.
> Don't you hear it
> Praying and sighing and groaning for wholeness?
> Sighing and whispering: wholeness,
> wholeness, wholeness?
> An arduous, tiresome difficult journey
> towards wholeness.
> *God who gives us strength of Body,*
> *make us whole.*
>
> Wholeness of persons: well-being of individuals.
> The cry for bodily health and spiritual
> strength is echoed from person to
> person, from patient to doctor.

It goes out from a soul to its pastor.
We, busy, "normal" people: we are sick.

We yearn to experience wholeness in
our innermost being:
In health and prosperity, we continue
to feel un-well, unfilled or half-filled.
There is hollowness in our pretend well-being:
Our spirits cry out for the well-being of
the whole human family . . .
We are all parts of each other,
We yearn to be folded into the fullness of life—together . . .

God who give us strength of body,
Make us whole.[1]

When I heard this prayerful conversation between the human need for
wholeness and the *God who gives us strength of body* for the first time, it stopped
me in my tracks. It accosted me as though I had been running away from
something that should have been as natural to me as breathing—something
on which my very life depended. I realized that my thirst for life, my hunger
for well-being and for healing from the brokenness that so permeated my
existence as black and as woman in American culture, was part of that same
yearning for wholeness that echoes from across the globe. And to my surprise
and dismay, I realized that the busyness of life had dulled my hearing to their
cries and to the yearning within my own soul.

I dare say that many of us have been longing for wholeness—wholeness
of body, mind, and spirit. Restlessness rattles us at the core of our being, though
the source of our discontent often remains obscure. Even when our individual
lives are at peace, the un-wholeness of our world leaves us restless—yearning
for a time when all persons might be well:

when the genocidal cries of suffering will end and peace will take its
rightful place;

when cosmic unrest will give way to re-creation

and God's image in each person will be revealed and not denied.

No doubt, we have sensed the Spirit of God beckoning us toward
wholeness, but we are preoccupied with our day-to-day joys and struggles—
what our poet calls the busyness of life—and we find little time to answer the
call.

In this Luke 10 text, Jesus calls seventy women and men away from their busy lives and sends them out to heal the un-well *and* to announce, *"the kingdom of God has come near."* This story found only in Luke's Gospel reminds us that the prophetic and liberating ministry of Jesus was not limited to Jesus alone or to the twelve or to the people of Jesus' time. No, Luke reminds us that Jesus beckons all those who follow him to prophetically announce the emergence of this new reality and kinship community.

Luke introduces us to seventy ordinary people sent to proclaim that the *kingdom of God has come near,* seventy ordinary people with limited preparation and whose only instructions were to choose a partner and go:

Go without money or a change of clothing or sandals [or a cell phone, as might be our practice today].

Go with healing power in your hands and words of peace dripping from your lips.

Do not get distracted by those whom you pass along the road, lodge with those who are willing to receive you and eat what is set before you as proper compensation for your work.

Seventy common folk were chosen as we are chosen and sent forth to proclaim good news, armed solely with the promise of the kingdom and the courage to say, "Yes, send me, I'll go." Luke never tells us their names, but perhaps among the seventy were the men, women, and children whom Jesus fed with two fish and five loaves of bread at the banquet on the plains, who had been so compelled by his teachings that they followed him out to the countryside without packing a lunch for themselves. Or perhaps the boy who had been possessed with a demon, or Jarius's daughter resurrected from the dead, or their parents or others whom Jesus healed were among the seventy who responded to Jesus' invitation. Or maybe the seventy included our sister with the issuance of blood who had spent so much of her life fighting a seemingly incurable disease and chose to spend the remainder of her life following Jesus.

What we do know is that they were seventy women and men who powerfully proclaimed the emergence of a new reality in the towns and villages in which they ministered. They were persons like you and me, uncertain about what lay before them, with no guarantee of security or success, but they were bound together by a common thread: They were willing to go and proclaim in word and deed that *the kingdom of God has come near.*

The nearness of God's kingdom seems shrouded in mystery in our day and age. For some, it is an obscure biblical concept with no grounding in reality, situated in a world in which technology and scientific innovations rule the day. Belief in God's kingdom has been replaced by what Rubem Alves calls *humanistic messianism*—the kind of thinking that wants us to believe that if you cannot see it, it does not exist; if it is does not appear humanly possible, then it cannot be done.[2] Those who embrace this way of thinking believe that human ingenuity alone can save our world; that we should put our trust in what is visible and tangible, eliminating the need for God and for religious faith of any form. There is no place for mystery, for faith, for hope, for God.

Others believe that the kingdom of God is that otherworldly place— that distant land and ultimate destination for those who name the name of Jesus; the *sweet by and by* about which the hymn writer sings, "In the sweet by and by we shall meet on the beautiful shore."[3] This image admonishes us to endure suffering, promising us that all will be well in our heavenly home. And while the prospect of heaven may be compelling, this image is grossly inadequate for those who suffer daily from the harsh realities of life; those who are starving, homeless, or daily hunted by annihilating regimes; those who are raped and abused and live in fear each day of their lives. *They* dare not wait until the *sweet by and by* to find relief.

When we look closely, another image emerges: an image woven throughout the biblical witness and offered to us in our text today. The reality of the kingdom, Jesus reveals, cannot be found in humanistic messianism or in otherworldly thinking but in Jesus' instruction to the seventy: "Whenever you enter a town . . . cure the sick who are there, and say to them, 'The kingdom of God has come near to you.'"

In other words, the healing and delivering work that these seventy ordinary people performed brought the kingdom of God near to us—so close that those who were broken could feel the heartbeat of God reviving their souls again; so palpable that its pulsating rhythm filled the cosmos as women, children, and men who had been sick, unwell, and less than whole discovered how radically God loves them.

As we witness their health springing forth, we become acutely aware that the kingdom of God is not a destination to which we travel, but a present reality in which we live: a reality that is taking shape in the concreteness of human existence—the domain of God, right here, in our midst; a commonwealth or kinship community in which all are welcomed and none are relegated to the margins; a kinship community in which God endows ordinary people with extraordinary power so that the just and life-affirming world which God envisions might come to full fruition.

"The kingdom of God has come near to you," they proclaimed, affirming with every word, every touch, every miracle that God is giving shape to a new reality that negates every form of injustice and oppression, every manner of disease, every annihilating force, not in some distant land far away but right in the midst of our day-to-day lives. This is the reality that began to take shape as Jesus identified himself as "the One whom God anointed to bring good news to the poor, to proclaim release to the captives, and recovery of sight to the blind; to let the oppressed go free, and to proclaim the year of the Lord's favor" (Luke 4:18-19).

This is the reality that was taking shape amid the marches and protests of the 1960s, as persons who experienced the sting of oppression joined hands with others who were committed to a just and liberating society for all persons and spoke truth to the powerful of our land. It takes shape among the scholarly women from the Women's Center at the University of Ghana who make their way into the mountain villages to talk with their sisters about HIV, AIDS, and sexual violence. It takes shape among grandparents who rescue and raise their grandchildren when the parents cannot; among foster parents, mentors, and surrogates who are willing to pour into our children that which gives them strength of body, mind, and spirit; and among teachers and school administrators whose care for their students will not permit them to lapse into mediocrity. It takes shape among caregivers who nurture and heal, missionaries, relief workers, and numerous others who travel to the most devastating regions of our nation and world—to the places where starvation and disease abound, where war and the threat of war are daily realities, where natural disaster robs persons and communities of the security that they once knew. The kingdom is taking shape among those who walk the hallowed halls of divinity schools, listening intently to the voices of the scholars and practitioners who have paved the way, who have shared hopes and dreams together as they seek to learn what it means to live together as human family. It takes shape as we extend our hands to congregations and agencies committed to nurturing faith and meeting the concrete needs of those who struggle and, yes, among those who permit the transformative possibilities that these experiences create to make us harvesters for God's vineyard.

Therefore, when we pray, "Thy kingdom come, they will be done on earth as it is in heaven," we are not simply asking that God set right what has gone wrong with the world, but that God might empower us to become agents of hope and deliverance against the principalities and powers that would keep us unwell.

"Whenever you enter a town and its people welcome you, eat what is set before you, cure the sick who are there, and say to them the kingdom of God has come near to you" because "The harvest is plentiful, but the laborers are few."

The harvest is plentiful . . .
those who have been ripened by the circumstances of life,
yearning and praying that someone somewhere would extend a hand
or whisper a prayer
or shed a tear *and* wail out a lament
or offer a morsel *and* safe place to lay their heads;
to relieve their distress, their grief, and unrest.

The harvest is plentiful . . .
men and women whose lives are exhausting:
tired of drinking and drugging and dragging,
tired of cussing and crying,
tired of existing but not living,
feeling that there is no way out,
and not at all sure that this life-giving message of Jesus is for them.

The harvest is plentiful . . .
among those who are looking for any glimmer of hope:
women and men, boys and girls,
believing themselves to be nothing
because they were told that they would never amount to anything
by those who should have been securing their well-being.

The harvest is plentiful . . .
among women and men who possess all of the trappings of success
but cannot stop searching;
searching for something or someone to hold on to,
seeking to fill the void where laughter once lived,
scouring the ruins of their lives for hidden treasure,

listening for a voice amidst the chaos,
and reaching out into the darkness for something that is Holy;
some Divine presence,
for a Love that is sure
for someone who is God.

The harvest is plentiful . . .
children, women, and men,
fathers and mothers, old and young,
all falling and failing,
all crying and dying,
all grasping and gasping,
all reaching, groaning, moaning, straining for Wholeness

The harvest is plentiful . . . but the laborers are few.

Let me admit that being a laborer in God's vineyard is no easy task. "See, I am sending you out like lambs into the midst of wolves," is what Jesus says. Yet, despite the danger, Jesus compels us to go, not because he wants us to be devoured but because the coming of God's kinship community and the ongoing emergence of this new reality are dependent upon laborers who are willing to venture into the unknown; laborers and harvesters who are willing to confront every negating and annihilating force and live as an expression of God's presence in our world today; laborers locking hearts and hands with other like-minded persons, believing beyond any shadow of doubting that the wolves *shall not* devour us and we will reap a bountiful harvest, to the glory of God!

That is what the seventy discovered. Upon their return, they reported, with joy, that at the name of Jesus the sick were cured, demonic spirits submitted to their command, and lives were changed. In response, Jesus said, "I beheld Satan as lightning fall from heaven. Behold, I give unto you power to tread on serpents and scorpions, and over all the power of the enemy, and nothing shall by any means hurt you."

And then we hear it! That blessed assurance that no power or principality or political entity or murderous regime can restrain the reality that is taking shape right in the midst of us today. And so we pray, even the more, "Thy kingdom come, Thy will be done," and we embark upon that "arduous, tiresome, difficult journey toward wholeness."

We believe with the utmost confidence that the kingdom of God must come, and...

There is no sin that can block it,
No power that can stop it,
No authority that can detain it,
No boundary that can contain it,
No threat than can destroy it,
No demon that can devour it,
No muzzle that can stifle it,
No regime that can annihilate it,
No level of despair that can negate it,
No toxic spirit that can contaminate it.
It is so palpable that we can almost touch it,
So close that we can sense its heartbeat,
And before we know it, our hearts begin to beat in sync
with the heart of God and God's hope for creation.

The kingdom of God has come near to us, and its ongoing emergence is the fruit of our labor. As we study and do the hard work of building community, as we transcend the social and religious boundaries that would keep us apart, as we offer the gift of well-being to others *and* receive the same in return, we bear the fruit of this new reality, *to the glory of God!*

"Whenever you enter a town and its people welcome you, eat what is set before you; cure the sick who are there and say to them, 'The Kingdom of God has come near to you.'"

Help Wanted: Harvesters for God's Vineyard

Now, let's get to work!

"Help Wanted: Harvesters for God's Vineyard!" was preached at Wake Forest University Divinity School's Fall Orientation Worship, Winston-Salem, North Carolina, on August 25, 2011.

Notes

1. Desmond Tutu, "Reflections on Wholeness," in *An African Prayer Book*, ed. Tutu (New York: Doubleday, 1995) 110–13.

2. Rubem A. Alves, *A Theology of Human Hope* (New York: Corpus Publications, 1969).

3. *New National Baptist Hymnal*, music by Joseph P. Webster, words by Sanford F. Bennett, 1868, hymn #447.

Chapter Twenty-One

Under God's Wings
(Luke 13:31-35)

Gwen Brown

2010 Recipient of the Addie Davis Award for Outstanding Leadership in Pastoral Ministry

Is there anyone here who knows that even when trouble comes, even when things are bleak and dark, the Bible says God will deliver us from our troubles, our joy comes in the morning? And if we know that God is a God who is able to keep us from falling, we need to give our God praise. If God has done anything for you, if God has been good to you, you need to put your hands together and give our God some praise all over the sanctuary.

For when I think about the goodness of God and all that God has done for me, my soul rejoices. I thank God for blessing me. I thank God for keeping me. I thank God for waking me up this morning and starting me on my way.

As God's people, we know that the Lord's hands are upon us. We know that we can take refuge under God's wings. Many of the Old Testament references to wings are descriptions of the cherubim in the holy of holies—that location in the temple that was a place of safety, a place of refuge. Other Old Testament references to wings also suggest the idea of refuge. In the book of Ruth, when Boaz was commending Ruth for her loyalty to her mother-in-law, he made mention of wings: "May the LORD repay you for what you have done. May you be richly rewarded by the LORD, God of Israel, under whose wings you have come to take refuge" (Ruth 2:12). The psalmist refers to wings as well. In Psalm 91, we read, "He will cover you with his feather, and under his wings you will find refuge; his faithfulness will be your shield and rampart" (v. 4). Yes, we are under God's wings, and there under God's wings we will find protection and refuge.

In the text for today in Luke 13, we find that our Lord's heart was grieved because of all the unbelief and all the rebellion he had encountered. Jesus had been teaching and preaching to a group of people who wanted to embrace their own way of living. But Jesus knows their plight. Jesus sees what lies ahead for the Jewish nation. And in this passage, Jesus seems more anguished than angry. Jesus is like that mother or father whose heart breaks when they witness their children going down the wrong path. When mom and dad realize that no matter what they say, no matter how much they pray, their children will just keep breaking their hearts. They are consumed with anguish, not anger.

To explain his own anguish, Jesus uses the image of the hen and her chicks, an image that would have been familiar to his listeners. He says, "How often I have wanted to gather your people just as a hen gathers her chicks under her wings." The Jewish people would have seen such a scene, a mother hen rounding up her chicks when she sees danger coming, drawing them close. Barbara Brown Taylor describes that mother hen as looking ready to spit fire if anyone threatens her babies.[1]

So, despite the fact that in this text the Pharisees warn Jesus that he is in danger, in reality, they are the ones in danger. And Jesus, compassionate, brokenhearted Jesus, had a message for them, a message we still must hear today: "Repent and be saved." For the Pharisees, just like some of us today, refuse to heed his call. Like wayward children, those Pharisees will not hear Jesus' words. They won't listen.

There is an insurance commercial that I often see. The scene is a two-car accident. One man involved in the fender bender has his insurance representative on the scene in seconds. The other man has different insurance, and he calls out for help as he and his son are waiting by the side of the road. And instead of a representative, his mother shows up, standing nearby talking on her telephone. His young son says, "Look, Dad, there's Grandma," and he replies, "I know who it is." Then Grandma says, "Six callers ahead of us, Jimmy." The man shakes his head and says, "You're not helping."[2] But listen, God's people: under God's wing, there is no one ahead of you in line. When you call upon the name of the Lord, God is always present. God is a very present help in time of need, very present.

I love that even though the people did not listen to Jesus' words, he did not change his message. And the message does not change for our children or for us. Unless we repent and are saved, we will be left desolate. In that day, the city and temple would soon be destroyed. The people scattered. Even knowing what was to come, Jesus was consistent in his message, and we too, especially as parents, must be consistent. We can't give up on our children. We must fight hard so that the enemy does not kill, steal, and destroy their future. We cannot change the message just because we do not get along with them. For if we give in and give up, they will be left desolate and will never reach the place to which God is calling them. We must be consistent in our message just as Jesus was.

If you have ever loved someone that you could not protect, then you understand the depth of Jesus' lament. All you can do is open your arms. You cannot make anyone walk into them. But you stand there in the most vulnerable posture in the world—wings spread open, breast exposed, waiting.[3] If you love, this is how you stand.

Look back at the text and be encouraged. The passage tells us that there is a future for Israel, for a time will come when their Messiah will return and surely will be recognized and received by the people. At some point, they will say, "Blessed is he that cometh in the name of the Lord" (Luke 13:35). These were words used by some at Jesus' triumphal entry into Jerusalem (Luke 19:38), but there will not be ultimate fulfillment of Jesus' prophecy until he returns in glory.

Today I offer you this encouragement: there is a future for you and for me—if we repent and are saved we will not be left desolate. We will see the goodness of the Lord in the land of the living, that is, if we keep our words filled with truth and not change the message. God will deliver us, and we will not be left desolate.

Jesus tells us that we are protected from danger just like those chicks. And for those we love, we will go the extra mile, as did the hen, to ensure that our children, our family, our friends are safe from all threats. We will share with them the message—and we will not change the message when the pressure is on.

Today, God's people, perhaps you are here, and you are filled with worry. I say to you—do not worry, for the Lord is working all things together for your good. If you have a situation that seems even now unbearable, unshakable, unmovable, you may not know what the future holds, but you know who holds the future. Some call him Wonderful Counselor, Mighty God, Prince of Peace, Everlasting Savior. I call him Jesus—Jesus. He is the one who paid it all on Calvary. They did horrible things to Jesus, and he knew that they would. Yet his time line, his mission and ministry, were not based on people's treatment of him.

In Luke 13, we find Jesus in Perea and Galilee, a land ruled by Herod Antipas, the son of Herod the Great. The Pharisees find him there. They want Jesus back in their own territory, so that they can watch him and ultimately trap him. So these religious leaders try to frighten him. They say to him, "Go! Get away from here, because Herod wants to kill you." The Pharisees' words were believable, for Herod was perplexed by Jesus' ministry. He was fearful that John the Baptist, whom he had murdered, had come back from the dead (Luke 9:7-9). Later, Herod would express that he had long desired to meet Jesus, to hear from Jesus, to see Jesus perform a miracle (Luke 23:8). But at this point in Jesus' journey, Herod was threatening to kill Jesus, at least according to the Pharisees, and their words were undoubtedly true, or Jesus would not have answered as he did.

In response to the Pharisees' warnings, Jesus uses a bit of "holy sarcasm." He compares Herod to a fox, an animal not held in high esteem by the Jews. Known for its cunning, the fox was surely an apt image by which to describe crafty Herod. But Jesus was in God's hands. Our Lord was not afraid of the danger that Herod presented. Jesus had work to do, and he would accomplish it. He was following a "divine timetable," and nothing could harm him. He was doing the will of God, according to God's schedule. Even Herod Antipas could not hinder the purposes of God. Quite the contrary. In the end, the Lord's enemies helped him fulfill the will of God.

The word of the Lord for us today tells us:

1. Our Lord's heart was grieved as he saw unbelief and rebellion all around him. For us, today, there is still rebellion and unbelief all around us, but like Jesus we must keep the message we share filled with truth and love.

2. Our Lord sobbed tears of anguish not anger. He showed us that we cannot let the sun set on our wrath. We cannot live out of anger, for when we do that we give room for the enemy to come and kill, steal, and destroy lives.

3. Our Lord's heart was broken. We too live with broken hearts, but we know that God will wipe away our tears, will keep on holding our hands, and we can stay safe under his wings.

4. Jesus chose a hen to describe God's love and protection. As Barbara Brown Taylor reminds us,

> A hen is what Jesus chooses, which—if you think about it—is pretty typical of him. He is always turning things upside down, so that children and

peasants wind up on top while kings and scholars land on the bottom. He is always wrecking our expectations of how things should turn out by giving prizes to losers and paying the last first. So of course he chooses a chicken, which is about as far from a fox as you can get. That way the options become very clear: you can live by licking your chops or you can die protecting the chicks.[4]

Today we celebrate God's goodness, for we know that God has his hands on us. We are under God's wing. God will see us through. God will wipe away our tears. God has promised to care for us, and so even now, if we are feeling down and just can't seem to find peace in our lives, we need to lift our hands up high and know that God will provide. And we give God praise. We are not ashamed of the gospel of Jesus Christ.

If you are feeling alone, feeling like you don't know what to do, you can start by giving God praise, for you see, things might not be what you want them to be, but they are not what they used to be. Just in case you need a reason why God deserves your praise, let me give you a few:

You can praise God because God answers your prayers.
You can praise God because God crowns you with love and compassion.
You can praise God because God delivers you from evil.
You can praise God because God equips you with what you need.
You can praise God because God gives you peace.
You can praise God because God will never leave nor forsake you.
You can praise God because God orders your steps in his word.
You can praise God because God quenches your thirst.
You can praise God because God redeems your life from the pit.
You can praise God because God understands your troubles and values every aspect of you.
You can praise God because God woke you up this morning.

If you have something for which to give God praise, open your mouth and with a loud voice, give our God some praise for how God keeps blessing you over and over again. For we are under the wings of God, and that is a safe place for us to be! Amen.

"Under God's Wings" was preached at Cornerstone Church, Snellville, Georgia, on February 24, 2013.

Notes

1. Barbara Brown Taylor, "As a Hen Gathers Her Brood," *Christian Century,* 25 February 1986, 201.

2. State Farm Insurance commercial.

3. Taylor, "As a Hen Gathers Her Brood," 201.

4. Ibid.

Chapter Twenty-Two

Journey to the Well of Reconciliation

(John 4:1-30, 39-42)

Veronice Miles
1999 Recipient of the Addie Davis Award for Excellence in Preaching

Our narrative is found in the Gospel of John, and might have been considered an incidental encounter between two people who met at a well one day, except for the forty-two verses that John devotes to it. John alone tells this story, inviting us to consider the details of Jesus' conversation with a woman of Samaria and its implications for our lives today. So what is John up to?

One of the interesting distinctions about the Gospel of John is that the writer, whom many believe to be John the Son of Zebedee, is transparent about his theological convictions and his commitment to affirming Jesus as the long-anticipated Messiah. As you might recall, John begins his Gospel with a declaration about Jesus' identity and ministerial purpose—who he is and what he has come to do: "In the beginning was the Word, and the Word was with God, and the Word was God. All things came into being through him, and without him not one thing came into being. What has come into being in him was life, and the life was the light of all people" (1:1-4).

Jesus is the *Word,* John emphatically tells us. He was *with* God in the beginning and is the embodiment *of* God so that *all people* might be reconciled *to* God. John leaves no questions about his beliefs. In fact, he makes it clear that Jesus' life and ministry, his words and deeds, his teaching and chance encounters are all intended to reconcile human persons with God—to link the human heart to the heart of God so that we might invite others into this divine fellowship. Jesus is the agent and source of reconciliation with God.

Reconciliation is the concern in our text today as we witness this unlikely encounter between Jesus, whom John calls the Messiah, and a woman of Samaria, a people with whom the Jews had been in contentious relationship for centuries.

Historically, the Samaritans were a conglomerate of many nations whom Shalmaneser, the Assyrian king, settled in Samaria when he conquered and exiled the northern kingdom of Israel (2 Kings 17). Though the inhabitants represented multiple nations and religious beliefs, the God of the Hebrew people still possessed the land itself, which meant that all who inhabited this geographic location called Samaria were required to fulfill Israel's commandment to worship the God of Israel alone.

This commandment created a dilemma for the new inhabitants of Samaria because, though exiled from their homelands, many of them held fast to their religious beliefs and worship practices, worshiping their own gods, the deities of their homeland, and maintaining their own customs. And while some also worshiped the God of Israel, YHWH was simply one among the many gods that they worshiped.

The Hebrew people rejected the Samaritans, including those who worshiped the God of Israel, and claimed the same ancestors, citing YHWH's commandment as justification for their decisions: "you shall not worship other gods or bow yourself to them or serve them or sacrifice to them" (2 Kings 17:35).

In the eyes of the Hebrew people, the Samaritans' understanding of God was incomplete, and their shrine to YHWH on Mt. Gerizim was not the true location for worship, despite the fact that both groups worshiped the God of Abraham, Isaac, and Jacob and both anticipated the Messiah who would come from God. The tension between these two groups intensified when the Jewish military destroyed the temple on Mt. Gerizim about 130 years before the encounter between Jesus and the Samaritan woman in our text today. In fact, no self-respecting Jewish teacher would be seen speaking with a woman of Samaria.

This climate exists between the Jews and Samaritans as an unsuspecting woman of Samaria begins her journey to the well to draw water for the day and meets Jesus at the well. Their communities had been at odds for centuries.

I rehearse this historical conflict because as much as I want to give this woman a name and make her familiar to us, I feel compelled to stand within the tension that her life reveals: her identity as woman, as grieving woman with no husband, as a woman who appears to stand alone, as a Samaritan woman in want of water to nourish her soul.

We meet her today in the city of Sychar about forty miles north of Jerusalem. The city sits right between Mt. Gerizim and Mt. Ebal—right between the two disputed worship locations—and is in many ways emblematic of the tension between the Jews and the Samaritans; a tension mirrored in the conversation between this woman of Samaria and Jesus whom John calls the Messiah.

Hear her story: She has just completed the morning chores, which took much longer than she had anticipated. Rinsing her hands with the last bit of water, this woman of Samaria gathers her water pots and begins her daily journey to the well. She is usually up and ready at the break of dawn, gathering empty vessels, making sure that the children are sound asleep and that all is well in her home. But today, things are a bit out of sorts.

We are not sure if one of the children became ill, if she overslept and missed the rooster's crow, or if, in light of her most recent tragedy, she just decided to begin her work a little later than usual. Whatever the reason, it is already noon, the sun is hot, and she must make the journey alone. *No sister* to walk with her in the cool of the morning, to laugh and talk and share juicy tidbits about the latest goings-on in their small town of Sychar. *No friend* with whom to share her grief or hear a word of encouragement. Today she walks alone, reflecting upon her life and asking once again when this period of struggle will end.

Life has been difficult for this sister. Her first husband died a few years ago, and she married a second time. But before she could even grasp what was happening to her, tragedy and loss struck again, silencing the laughter and song of her life and intensifying her pain. Now, grieving the deaths of four husbands and resisting the notion that she is somehow accursed, she is cautious, very cautious about marrying again. For, although she knows herself as one whom loves God, she cannot help but wonder if the talk is true—if somehow God has forgotten her.

People murmur that she has the touch of death—that she and all who dwell with her are cursed, and she is tempted to believe them. Others, *even those of us centuries removed from her grief,* suppose that she is a harlot or a woman deserving of public disdain, refusing to believe that life could ever be this difficult. But contrary to what some may believe, this woman of

Samaria is no harlot, no serial divorcée, no loose and scandalous woman who does not know God, but a sister left empty by tragedy and loss.

Water pot in hand, she comes to the well, an open vessel in want of water *and* desperately needing to be filled.

She has been empty for so long, thirsty in the very depths of her soul, bone dry and parched in her ability to dream for so long, that she has almost forgotten what it means to drink, what it means to be content, what it means to experience real joy, *what it means to be complete!*

"My God, my God," she must have thought, "why have you forsaken me?" She wanted and desperately needed to be whole again!

Wholeness is difficult when our lives are fragmented—when we dress up so nice and greet people with a smile, all the while aching inside,
when we go to work each day carrying the weight of the world on our shoulders,
yet never bending over or breaking down,
water pot balanced on our head, because we have been taught to carry water even if we do not know how to drink.

Singing and *praying,*
testifying and *prophesying,*
teaching and *preaching,*
saving and *preserving,*
nurturing and *guiding*
while our own souls remain in want of water.

Wholeness is difficult when we hold secrets too dangerous to tell,
life stories too painful to remember,
scars etched so deeply upon our hearts
that it seems they will never heal.

Wholeness is difficult when devaluation shrouds our existence:
be a woman, they tell us, but not too womanish,
be intelligent but hide your competence,
be spiritual but not prophetic,
be strong but not the leader,
stand in the midst but do not speak.

Wholeness is difficult when we are always struggling to defend ourselves...
against negating representations that some call normative,
against dehumanizing rhetoric that some call art,
against subordinating proclamation that some call holy,
against gender marginalization that some say God requires
against racial discrimination that some say does not exist.

Wholeness is difficult when you are a Samaritan woman,
a grieving woman,
a scorned and scarred woman,
hated and marginalized,
deemed *perpetually* unclean,
and unworthy of reconciliation with God.

She has heard it all before but refuses to concede that wholeness is impossible!

And then she sees him: Jesus, sitting at the well—this *rabbi/ teacher/preacher/prophet* whom many are already calling the Messiah, tired from his travels yet nourished by manna that comes from God—sitting there as though anticipating her arrival, asking her to give him a drink and then declaring that he can give her water that will quench her thirst forever.

"How could this be true?" she thinks as she listens to this man with no bucket with which to draw from the well.

"Those who drink of the water which I will give them will never be thirsty," says Jesus. "The water that I will give will become in them [will become in you . . . will become in us] a spring of water gushing up to eternal life."

"Could it be," she thinks, "that this man can give me water more enduring and everlasting than the spring beneath Jacob's well? Water from a source more potent than the everlasting spring that has sustained my community for thousands of years? Living water, he called it, that will quench my thirst from the inside out and create a spring that will never run dry!"

While she does not yet grasp the nature of this *living water*, the prospect of never having to make the journey from her village to the well again, of *never* needing to balance that large water pot on her head again, of *deleting* one more thing from her busy day is extremely appealing to this woman of Samaria.

Of course—and the reader knows this before she does—Jesus is not really talking about physical water. He is inviting her, and he is inviting us, to experience the life-giving and nurturing presence of the Holy Spirit, reconciling us to God—linking our lives with the life of God, not conditioned upon our national origin, gender, race, ethnicity, social location, identity, or what other people think about us or the choices that we make.

Living Water that comes from God, potent enough to mend our brokenness and sustain us in our times of loss and grief, so that our lives might flourish and testify to God's presence in our world today.

Living Water, gushing up in us as an everlasting reminder that we have been reconciled to God—we and *all peoples* of the earth. For this is the God who transcends cultural and religious boundaries so that we might know each other as sisters and brothers created in the image of a Creating God.

The power of this water to bind us together becomes clear when we consider the risks that Jesus and this woman of Samaria incurred simply because they spoke together in this public space. She is a woman of Samaria, and Jesus is a Jewish teacher—transgressors of the social and religious boundaries of their time.

She is acutely aware of the boundary that separates them as they encounter each other at the well; so aware that she can scarcely hear Jesus' invitation to imagine the day when the conflict over location—the argument over which mountain—will no longer matter: "But the hour is coming and is now here, when the true worshipers will worship [God] in spirit and truth, for [these are the types of worshipers that God seeks]" (4:23).

The time is now, Jesus proclaims, not in some distant future that we call the *sweet by and by*, not at the completion of all things—the last days or eschatological future—but right here in the concreteness of human existence! *The hour is coming and is now here.*

As persons who endeavor to worship God in this present age, we are also aware of the many schisms that keep us divided:

the attitudes and dispositions of heart,
the prejudices and stereotypes,
the insecurities and fears,
the ideologies and claims of superiority.

And, as was true among the ancient Jews and Samaritans, we struggle to understand what it might mean to accept that we are all God's people, called to worship God in spirit and in truth. *To worship God in spirit* means acknowledging our soulish connection with God and surrendering our hearts to the One who can change us from the inside out:

God, who heals our wounded places and rescues us from annihilation,
lifts us when we are falling and showers us with mercy when we falter,
the One who shelters us with grace when we least deserve it
and emboldens us to hope when we can see no way out.

To worship God in spirit is to match our hearts to the heart of God—to
sense its rhythm and quietly permit our heartbeat to pick up the cadence
that has been pulsating throughout creation from the very beginning: Spirit
to spirit, heart to heart, pulse to pulse. As we sense God's presence in us,
the very presence of the Holy Spirit, we come to know what we must know:
that we are called and commissioned to become a practical reflection of
God's presence in the world:

to exemplify God's compassionate care,
to mend the brokenness in our world,
and open our arms to those who desperately
need a cool and refreshing drink to enliven their souls again
because to love as God loves is the *embodiment of truth.*

That is what Jesus is trying to say to the woman at the well and to those
of us who hear him today. When we match our hearts to the heart of God,
we worship God in spirit, and when we live as a reflection of God's presence
in the world, we worship God in truth. "The hour is coming and is now
here, when the true worshipers will worship [God] in spirit and truth."

Jesus demonstrates the timeliness of his message by the reconciling love
that he offers this woman of Samaria:

Jesus never called the woman a Samaritan miscreant,
never denied her living water on the grounds of her womanhood or
Samaritan ethnicity,
never spoke a word that diminished her worth,
never deemed her a sinner despite our tendency to condemn her.

No. He simply narrated her story back to her so that she would know
that he heard her and knew her. He spoke her secrets back to her because
he loved her; transcended the barriers of ethnic superiority and religiosity
in order to reveal that God's merciful grace cannot be constrained by person
or place, nationality, ethnicity, or religious tradition. And in that moment,

she was so filled with love and gratitude, so enlivened and empowered, that she could not hold her peace.

Leaving her water pots at the well, she returns to the city. I imagine her running back to the city and through the streets, beckoning all who would to come see a man. "Come see a man," she cries in the marketplace and in the streets, from house to house and in the fields, determined to proclaim *this* good news to all who would hear her. "Come see a man!" And they came . . . running to Jesus . . . sorely needing and desperately wanting the water that would never stop flowing!

We also come, in this hope-filled moment, as we sense the emptiness within our own souls and drink from this ever-flowing fountain. And as we take a sip of that cool and refreshing water, we feel the transforming power of the Holy Spirit synchronizing our hearts with the heart of God so that we might live as a reflection of God's presence in our world.

For this and more, we are thankful. Thank you, Jesus, for giving us this word of reconciliation to bind us together with our sisters and brothers. And thank you, our sister whose name we do not know, for proclaiming the good news of God's reconciling presence in your community and in our world today. We need this living water!

"Journey to the Well of Reconciliation" was preached at Baptist Women in Ministry's annual worship service, Bayshore Baptist Church, Tampa, Florida, on June 22, 2011.

Chapter Twenty-Three

Feel Your Hunger
(Acts 2:1-21)

Kyndall Rae Rothaus
2011 Recipient of the Addie Davis
Award for Excellence in Preaching

I have been reminded recently on more than one occasion that God answers prayer. But I would be the first to tell you that life experience has, for the most part, taught me exactly the opposite. God does *not* answer prayer most of the time—or at least God does not answer prayer in the way I want God to answer or on the timetable I expect. In fact, life can be so brutal that I forget to pray at all, or I choose not to pray for fear of being disappointed.

Sometimes I re-choose prayer by a sheer effort of my will. I discipline my practices in hopes that my faith will catch up. Other times I remember to pray because suddenly Grace plops down in my life like a bounding Tigger, as if to say, "I can't believe you didn't see me coming," and I am surprised all over again that Grace is real.

On the Day of Pentecost, Grace plopped down with a flourish and shocked the socks off everyone—so much so that you could not tell a Spirit-filled apostle from a drunken fool on the street, so the story goes. It was a confusing, throbbing, magnificent mess in which the Spirit of God was so conspicuous, so alive, so mobile, so awake and irresistible that the author of our text could only describe it by saying that the Spirit was like fire and like wind. All consuming, it sounded like the blowing of a violent wind that filled the whole house, and it looked like tongues of fire that rested on each of them.

I read this story and feel either hungry for God or frustrated at God, but I never feel satisfied. I am either hungry to experience God like that or frustrated because God never seems to show up that way anymore, and I am not the only one who feels this way. I see people reacting to hunger/frustration all the time. They either leave faith behind because they are fed up with God's seeming absence or they reduce faith down to something akin to spotting fairies—that is, they see the hand of God every time they get a good parking spot (Praise the Lord!) or when they pass a wreck on the highway (Praise the Lord! I've been spared!). Our tendency is to reject faith or mythologize faith—anything to escape the real-life collision of prayer and reality, where you seldom get what you ask for and occasionally get just what you need before you even think to ask.

Acts 2 makes it all seem so easy, like the Holy Spirit will just fly right down and baptize us by fire. The three-year cycle of the lectionary (which I will have you know leaves out certain biblical texts entirely) does us the great disservice of forcing us to read this very text every stinking year. It is exasperating because it makes you *want* the Spirit of God to show up powerfully, which of course it will not because everyone knows that the Spirit of God never cooperates with our calendars. The Spirit does its own thing—the wind blows where it will, the expression goes—and for all our manipulative tricks, we cannot get that thing under our control. We want the Spirit at our beck and call. The Spirit becks and calls at us instead, but you would have to be listening close to know it.

Madeleine L'Engle tells the story of being in a church service on a Pentecost Sunday in which the youth of the church were tasked with leading the entire worship experience. But the radical religious notions of the youth actually drove some people to stand up and walk out of an already small crowd in a sort of reverse-Pentecost experience. The adults could not understand the language of the youth, whether the Spirit resided in their tongues or not, and so there was a scattering rather than a gathering.[1] I would venture to guess that most church services on most Pentecost Sundays are not nearly that dramatic. Most Pentecost Sundays pass by usual smusual. Nobody gets up and walks out in a huff. Nobody is overcome by the Spirit of the Living God. We all go home, eat our Sunday meals, take our Sunday naps, and try not to think about our Monday mornings around the bend. Same. Story. As. Always.

But the preacher in me wants this to be a real Pentecost Sunday. If we are going to observe Pentecost, I want to see some spiritual fireworks. It isn't fair, if you ask me, for the church calendar to impose Pentecost Sunday on us, mere humans who do not get to choose when God moves.

Of course, the disciples in Jerusalem that day were not responsible for God's movement either. The only thing they were responsible for was showing up. They were responsible for gathering together, for waiting, and for praying, and those were the only meaningful jobs they had, which must have been maddening because there was no guarantee that waiting for the Lord was ever going to pay off, or take off, or whatever. They could cling to faith, or they could abandon faith, but there was not much they could be sure about, nothing concrete to do, and no way to control the outcome, and so they just huddled together and hoped.

"When the day of Pentecost came," says the text, "they were all together in one place." You get the sense that the only choice they were given ahead of time was either to be in that room or not be in that room, and apparently they all chose to be there, and when the Spirit arrived it passed up no one, and the rest is history.

I do not mean to suggest that the life of faith is a passive one. Choosing God, choosing faith, and choosing love again and again are some of the hardest decisions and biggest steps we will ever take. Yet we work ourselves into an anxious muddle when we start believing that our action causes God's movement. We either plague ourselves with guilt or lavish ourselves with praise depending on the direction of the Wind. Most of the spiritual choices we make in life are simply about showing up in those places where God is most likely to move. God is more likely to show up when I am extending hospitality to my neighbor than when I am gossiping to a friend. God is more likely to show up when I am praying than when I am watching commercials. God is more likely to show up in the silence than when my iPod is blaring. Even still, the Spirit of God is so alive it might just show when we least expect and when we are not trying to listen at all. Even still, the discipline of showing up in the right places is worth it in the long run.

Eugene Peterson wrote, "Worship does not satisfy our hunger for God—it whets our appetite."[2] His words haunt me. They suggest that this Pentecost story is not intended to be a satisfying story in any way. It is meant to make us hunger, to make us burn, to make us want. On an average day, I simmer down my need for God as much as possible because I would rather get by on my own. I turn down the volume on my want because I do not want to be disappointed. I hide from my hunger for God because I am just not sure God is all that interested in me anyway.

But on Pentecost Sunday, I let the tears of my longing flow. I open myself back up to hunger. I gather together with all of you. We huddle together, and we hope. It is rather maddening because there is not much we can be sure about, nothing concrete to do, and no way for us to control the outcome, but even still we show up. We wait. We tell stories, because everyone has at least one story where Grace caught them by surprise.

There is a line from noonday prayer in Macrina Wiederkehr's *Seven Sacred Pauses* that says, "Before we share our noonday meal, our deepest hungers let us feel."[3] In a well-fed country like this one, we do not like to feel our hunger. We are accustomed to feeding our bellies as soon as they begin to grumble, or we just go ahead and eat before we are hungry, just to stay on top of things. But before we share a noonday meal, our deepest hungers let us feel. What I mean is, what if we quit being afraid of our need for God? What if we weren't so skittish about being disappointed by God? What if we decided that every disappointment was in fact getting us closer to the truth of God, and although it is painful to have our idols shattered, it is not exactly a bad thing? But more important, what if we weren't so convinced that Grace has gone and hidden from us for good? What if we expected Grace to plop down in our lives at any moment, as if to say, "Didn't you see me coming?" What if hope isn't a waste? What if Grace is on its way, and we just do not know it yet? What if our everyday troubles and the looming tragedies do not get the last word in our lives and in our world? What if prayer is something God hears? What if it is not time for you to give up? What if the people around here will actually wait with us and not pass judgment? What if all this will be worth it in the end? We never know when the winds of the Spirit are going to start blowing, but I sure want to be there when it happens. And I hope we are all together in the same room when it does.

I would like to watch how Carolyn would jump and then laugh for joy when a tongue of fire rested on her head. I would like to see Isabel's hair blowing in the rushing wind, and I would enjoy hearing Taty speaking in another language, although, come to think of it, maybe the Spirit already visits us here more than we realize. Either way, you are the people I want to wait and pray and hope and dream with. Oh Spirit of the Living God, fall on us, we pray. Amen.

"Feel Your Hunger" was preached at Covenant Baptist Church, San Antonio, Texas, on Sunday, May 27, 2012.

Notes

1. Madeleine L'Engle, *The Irrational Season* (New York: Seabury Press, 1977) 144–145.

2. Eugene Peterson, *A Long Obedience in the Same Direction* (Downers Grove IL: Intervarsity, 2000) 2d ed., 56.

3. Macrina Wiederkehr, *Seven Sacred Pauses* (Notre Dame IN: Sorin Books, 2008) 102.

Chapter Twenty-Four

Construction Zone

(1 Corinthians 3:10-11, 16-23)

Karen Hatcher

2010 Recipient of the Addie Davis Award for Excellence in Preaching

The morning dawned clear and crisp. Most Saturdays I would have rolled over and drifted back to sleep, but not today. A number of church members, myself included, had volunteered to help construct Powhatan County's first Habitat for Humanity house. No matter that I did not know a two-by-four from a sheet of plywood; I was willing to play the apprentice. Donning a well-worn pair of jeans, I grabbed my hammer and set out for the building site, a wooded lot whose shade trees would provide welcome relief from the summer sun. Once there, I joined other willing workers around the foundation, which had already been laid, and listened attentively as the foreman divided us into teams and gave directions for our tasks. He was a seasoned professional with a vision for the finished structure and the expertise to realize it through the energy and gifts of those gathered. Walls were raised, and doors and windows framed to the high-pitched buzz of power saws, the rhythmic pounding of nails, and the light-hearted banter of those united in a common goal. At day's end we left tired, sore, and sweaty, satisfied that our work had passed inspection and gratified that those hallowed halls would soon be housing their new residents.

In the 1 Corinthians 3 text, we find a similar building project, but things are not going all that well for the Christians in Corinth. Having learned from Chloe's people (1:11) about growing dissension in the church he had planted, Paul pens a letter issuing an urgent appeal for unity. The apostle's earlier eighteen-month mission in Corinth had given him a good idea of the competitiveness, status seeking, and self-promotion that characterized the citizens of this bustling, cosmopolitan Roman colony. Conditioned by their culture, the fledgling congregation had allowed that same ethos to permeate the church. Now they were creating factions loyal to Paul, Apollos, or Peter, aligning themselves with these ministers of the gospel much as they would attach themselves to influential secular patrons to increase their social prestige. Paul deplores these divisions and sets about correcting their mistaken notions about the nature of their newly adopted religion. The Christian faith community was not merely another civic society but an entirely different kind of *ecclesia,* an assembly called to mirror the holiness of the God that had called them and set them apart for service (Lev 19:1-2). Addressing them as "saints, who have been sanctified in Christ Jesus," Paul implores them to become in practice the "holy ones" they already are by God's grace (1 Cor 1:2).

To help them recapture a sense of their true identity, he argues from analogy, comparing them first to God's field, cultivated by a succession of ministering "farmers," and later to Christ's body (1 Cor 12:27), composed of many members functioning together for the well-being of the whole. In our focal passage, Paul depicts them metaphorically as God's building with himself as *architecton.* Like a master builder, Paul had laid through his tireless preaching the church's one and only foundation—Jesus Christ, the crucified (1 Cor 2:2). Continued progress depended not only on ministerial leadership but also on teamwork, with each person contributing according to his or her gifts. The key was cooperation, not competition. But the Corinthians had been seduced by the egocentric wisdom of the world, and now they were beset by its inevitable detrimental consequences—self-glorification, jealousy, and discord—which threatened to derail the project. Now this is not just any edifice under construction, Paul goes on to say, but the very temple of God, so see to it that you build with care.

Scholar C. D. Buck cites the discovery of an Arcadian epigraph dating from the fourth century BCE that describes the construction and repair of the temple of the goddess Athena. In vocabulary that closely parallels Paul's wording, the epigraphy lists the various tasks meted out to the subcontractors and details the penalties for infractions, such as injuries to workers, property damage, and failure to finish on time.[1] The Corinthians are engaged in a similar sacred endeavor, and Paul issues a warning against shoddy, slap-dash workmanship that will not pass muster. Only those who have followed the specs can expect to receive their wages when inspection day rolls around.

Paul carries his metaphor a step farther, stating that the Corinthians are not only *building* God's temple, they *are* that temple, inhabited by the deity's very presence. "Do you not know that you are a sanctuary of God and that the Spirit of God dwells in you?" These "yous" are plural in the Greek. Later in his letter Paul will apply this same idea on a personal level, but here he speaks in corporate terms. Collectively, the Corinthian congregation is actually a cultic precinct where the Holy One has taken up residence. Unlike the adherents of pagan deities who flocked to stone temples made by human hands, Christians are living stones being fashioned into a new kind of temple, an eschatological community that worships the God in their midst in spirit and in truth. Given Paul's Jewish heritage and the fact that the Jerusalem temple was still standing—and would be until its destruction by the Romans in 70 CE—this claim was radical indeed. In his discussion with the Samaritan woman at the well regarding the proper site for worship, Jesus had told her, "Believe me, an hour is coming when you will worship the Father neither on [Mount Gerazim] nor in Jerusalem" (John 4:21). That time had come. In these last days, Yahweh's temple was a mobile home, and the Spirit's space was the *communio sanctorum*—the community of those God had sanctified.

If the Corinthians grasped the far-reaching implications of this assertion, they gave little indication of it. Rather, they were sabotaging the work of the Spirit with their quarreling, which not only had an impact on their social relationships but also undermined the very integrity of God's dwelling place. No less than the money-changers in the Jerusalem temple who incurred the wrath of Jesus, they were desecrating the house of God. Such contentiousness was a sure sign that the church was experiencing the insidious effects of the worldly wisdom the Corinthians prized so much—an "earthly, natural, demonic wisdom," the writer of James's epistle calls it—which produced disorder and stirred up conflict (Jas 3:15-16, NASB). The congregation was at best a loose collection of self-interested individuals, boasting in their sophistry and social connections, true products of Corinth's value system.

Anthony Thiselton describes the inhabitants of this wealthy, strategically located city as "a thrusting, ambitious, and competitive people."[2] The drive for success was evident everywhere—in the sports arenas of the biannual Isthmian Games, in the pervasive consumerism, in the pursuit of personal prestige, in the jockeying for economic power. Corinthians climbed the social ladder by networking, currying favor with influential patrons, or seeking the services of the spin doctors of the day—rhetoricians who broadcast their accomplishments to the public. Corinth was a magnet for entrepreneurs looking to transcend their humble origins and "make it" in a land of opportunity and freedom, and the mythos of the self-made human perpetuated individualism, autonomy, and self-sufficiency.

Sound familiar? This description bears a striking resemblance to the contemporary American landscape two thousand years later. Corinthian Christians were not the only ones guilty of dragging the world's way of thinking into the church. Shaped by the mantras of the mass media in an every-dog-for-himself culture, we American Christians have a tough time remembering that egocentrism is out of place in the Holy Place. Knowledge and power are the quintessential American idols. In fact, in this Age of Information, we proclaim that knowledge *is* power. Theologian Paul Tillich warns against the consequences of such a stance: "The wisdom of this world in all its forms cannot know God, and the power of this world with all its means cannot reach God. If they try it, they produce idolatry and are revealed in their foolishness, which is the foolishness of idolatry."[3]

The inescapable fact is that mortal reasoning has its limits. The truly wise are those who, like Socrates, are aware of their ignorance. It is senseless to boast in either what we know or whom we know. Either is inconsequential when set alongside God's knowledge and power. The old adage of the Greco-Roman philosophers is right after all, Paul says. "All things *do* belong to the wise"—to those, that is, with the wisdom to place themselves under God's patronage—for it is the divine Benefactor that makes them possessors of all things. That includes the self-effacing ministers who place themselves in the service of the congregation, who are not interested in gathering a fan base but rather in grounding the church in the truths of the gospel. It is by constructing on that immovable rock that we reveal our true wisdom, proving ourselves wise builders of a holy house capable of withstanding the tests of time and tempest.

Back in the 1990s, so-called shrink-swell soil was a hot topic among residents of upscale neighborhoods in Chesterfield County, where I currently live. Unbeknownst to them, their houses had been constructed on what geotechnical engineers term "expansive soil," which is composed of minerals capable of absorbing moisture. As the water volume increased, the soil would expand and exert pressure on the building, causing fissures in the foundation, torquing the framing and weakening the walls. The problem is a serious one. According to the American Society of Civil Engineers, in a typical year in the United States, expansive soils cause greater financial loss to property owners than earthquakes, floods, hurricanes, and tornadoes combined.[4] Moreover, the devastating results do not show up overnight. Instead, there is a slow, insidious process that goes undetected until the structure is severely damaged.

As with soils, so with souls. No less detrimental to God's house-church are the stresses caused by bloated egos swollen with the illusion of our own importance. Regular, careful inspection—or rather, introspection—will reveal the telltale rifts early on so that God's bonding agent can be applied. Love, with its other-centered orientation, is the repairer of breaches, seeping into the crevices of crumbling relationships, strengthening them like sacred cement. Love edifies. It is the mortar joining the living stones that make up the dwelling of God.

Directing and empowering the construction project is the Holy Spirit. To their credit, the Corinthians allowed the Spirit to move unfettered when they assembled, demonstrating in their *enthusiasm*[5] that they were indeed "possessed by their God," though perhaps, as Paul notes, in need of a few liturgical guidelines. Certainly worship shouldn't be a free-for-all. But I wonder if, in our penchant for order, we haven't gone to the other extreme in our worship services, setting the parameters so that the Spirit's movement among us is controlled, predictable, safe. We feel comfortable with a domesticated Spirit who passes through our midst like a gentle breeze, whispering to us as we sit quietly in our pews. We can handle that. But a Spirit who whips through a congregation with gale-force winds as at Pentecost is something altogether different, startling, unnerving. In reflecting on our desire to tame the divine Presence, Annie Dillard asks, "Does anyone have the foggiest idea what sort of power we so blithely invoke? Or, as I suspect, does no one believe a word of it? . . . It is madness to wear ladies' straw hats and velvet hats to church; we should all be wearing crash helmets. Ushers should issue life preservers and signal flares; they should lash us to our pews."[6] She has a point. If the church is a construction site, then we will be needing our hard hats. For the Spirit is always active, renovating the holy residence in surprising ways—breaking down a dividing wall here, putting on an addition there, installing a skylight to increase illumination from above, clearing out the rubble, patching up the cracks, and painting the place liberally with a love-based primer that covers over a multitude of sins. It is the great privilege of Christians to participate in this sacred task, to roll up our sleeves with an attitude of expectancy and openness to the Spirit's creative leading, encouraging one another as the divine blueprint gradually becomes concrete reality.

Situated among the ruins of Kabah in Mexico's Yucatan Peninsula is the still-impressive Palace of the Masks, a temple built by the Mayans to honor their rain god, Chac. The façade is composed of 250 virtually identical masks painstakingly carved by artisans to represent the deity. That is how I imagine the Holy Spirit's house, built up of living stones bearing the *imago Dei*—the image of God—each one a unique building block painstakingly sculpted into the likeness of Jesus Christ by the sanctifying power of the Spirit. Paul tells us that what really matters is our corporate identity as a people in union with God and with one another in Christ, as a shrine whose entrance bears the words "Belonging to the Lord" (Isa 44:5). Such a monument stands as a witness to the world, as hymnist Terry York suggests: "And should a seeker see the stones and ask what these rocks mean, / 'They are the church which our God owns and through which Christ is seen!'"[7]

This Grand Design is a work in progress gradually unfolding on multiple levels—in individual believers, in local congregations, in the church universal. As members of the Spirit's team, let us bring our team spirit and, laying aside our inflated egos, consecrate ourselves to a divine endeavor through which we are being built up even as we build on the rock-solid foundation already laid for us. Will you join us in building a habitat for the Holy One among humanity? If so, I will look for you in the construction zone. Amen.

"Construction Zone" was preached at Menokin Baptist Church in Warsaw, Virginia, on February 20, 2011.

Notes

1. C. D. Buck, cited in Raymond F. Collins, *First Corinthians*, ed. Daniel J. Harrington, Sacra Pagina Series 7 (Collegeville MN: The Liturgical Press, 1999) 149.

2. Anthony C. Thiselton, *First Corinthians: A Shorter Exegetical and Pastoral Commentary* (Grand Rapids MI: William B. Eerdmans Publishing Company, 2006) 9. See the introduction, 1–27.

3. Paul Tillich, "Chapter 15: All Is Yours," *The New Being* (New York: Charles Scribner's Sons, 1955).

4. "Expansive Soil and Expansive Clay: The Hidden Force Behind Basement and Foundation Problems," <http://geology.com/articles/expansive-soil.shtml> (accessed 9 February 2011).

5. The English word "enthusiasm" is derived from the Greek *enthousiazein*, to be inspired or possessed by a god (*enthous, entheos, en* [in] + *theos* [god]). It originally signified supernatural inspiration.

6. Annie Dillard, *Teaching a Stone to Talk* (New York: Harper and Rowe, 1982) 40–41.

7. Terry W. York, "Living Stones," in *The Baptist Hymnal* (Nashville: Convention Press, 1991) #353, words © 1986, Van Ness Press, Inc.

Chapter Twenty-Five

Rejoice, and Again I Say, Rejoice
(Philippians 4:4-8)

Teresa Pugh
2005 Recipient of Addie Davis
Award for Outstanding Leadership
in Pastoral Ministry

Back in the 1980s, songwriter Bobby McFerrin composed a little song called "Don't Worry, Be Happy." Remember the words?

> In every life we have some trouble
> When you worry you make it double
> Don't worry, be happy.
>
> Ain't got no place to lay your head
> Somebody came and took your bed
> Don't worry, be happy
> The landlord say your rent is late
> He may have to litigate
> Don't worry, be happy.[1]

This song reminds me that a lot of the time we worry about things we cannot control. We allow those worries to control us. When I am worried, I often have to quote to myself the Serenity Prayer by Reinhold Niebuhr:

God grant me the serenity
to accept the things I cannot change;
courage to change the things I can
and wisdom to know the difference.[2]

Many things come in our lives to steal our joy. Unexpected sickness, the loss of a job, the death of a family member, miscommunication in our closest relationships, and the list goes on. But I have come to tell you to *rejoice, and again I say, rejoice.*

In Philippians 4, we discover that Paul knows the heartaches and headaches that the Philippians are facing. He knows that they are aware of his imprisonment and are concerned that they too may face that same fate for being a Christian. Paul chooses words with which to encourage his friends not to lose hope. He encourages them not to look behind but to look ahead. Paul reminds them that they may encounter false teachers who will teach their own doctrine instead of teaching the truth of Christ, and Paul admonishes them to stick together and be in one accord. But more than anything, he wants them to know that no matter what they are facing, there is still joy.

Paul calls the Philippians to rejoice and be full of joy. In the previous chapter, he focuses on rejoicing, and in chapter 4, he repeats this encouragement: *rejoice, and again I say, rejoice.* For Paul, nothing can keep him from rejoicing. Even the prison bars that enclose him cannot take away his joy. Even the death penalty he faces cannot destroy his praise. Paul's circumstances and his words remind his readers and remind us that our joy cannot be dependent upon our circumstances, but instead our joy is dependent upon our creator.

Yet Paul does not rejoice for the simple sake of rejoicing. Instead, he rejoices in the Lord, and he calls his readers and he calls us to rejoice in the Lord always. We may receive a pink slip at work, but we can rejoice knowing that the Lord is able to open new doors. We may get a negative report about our health, but we can rejoice because we know the healer, the one who brings wholeness not only to our bodies but to our minds, souls, and broken hearts. Paul's instructive words about rejoicing are reminders to keep our eyes on the prize and not get so caught up with the negatives of this world that we cannot see all the positives that only God can bring to us. We must be joyous in knowing that whatever we face, God can make a way out of no way. So *rejoice, and again I say, rejoice.*

In verse 5, Paul tells the Philippians that they must allow others to see their gentleness of spirit. Gentleness and kindness will draw others to the church, and indeed, the community should be able to see that God's church is a safe haven, a place of peace and kindness. God's people must exhibit a spirit of gentleness, one that shines through even in adverse times.

Also in verse 5, Paul writes that the Lord is near, and he reminds the Philippians to be mindful of the time, to pay attention to the unfolding of events around them. The psalmist echoes that same thought. In Psalm 30:5, the psalmist writes, "Weeping may endure for a night, but joy cometh in the morning." No matter what comes our way, we know that troubles do not last forever. In God's own time, joy shows up and shows out. We cannot get too caught up or bogged down with what is going on right now, for we know that joy is on the way. "Joy to the world, the Lord is come." Joy came first in the form of a newborn babe wrapped in swaddling clothing. Joy will come again when Christ returns as our triumphant king and lord. Joy is on his way. Remember the song: "This joy I have, the world didn't give it to me."[3] Joy is near. Christ is near. How do I know? Because he lives within my heart. Jesus promised us that he would never leave us nor forsake us. *Rejoice, and again I say, rejoice!*

In verse 6, Paul instructs the Philippians not to worry. Do not be anxious. Well, I can tell you that it is difficult at best not to be anxious when you feel the weight of the world rest upon your shoulders. Sometimes it is humanly impossible to sleep or to eat or to stay focused when so much of life appears to be in turmoil. And Paul says, "Do not worry." How can we do that? How can we not worry when others depend on us? How can we not worry when it seems that no one else cares and that we are the only one that can change things? How can we not worry and rejoice in times like these?

In Nehemiah 8:10, the prophet tells God's people that the joy of the Lord is their strength. The Jewish people wanted to mourn over the losses they had experienced, but Nehemiah instructs them that this is not the time to have pity party. Instead, it is a time of rejoicing. He assures the Jews that they will find their strength in God's delight and joy.

In verse 6 of Philippians 4, Paul provides insight about how the people might move past worry to a place of rejoicing. He instructs the Philippians to pray—not to pray those empty prayers but to say prayers of supplication and thanksgiving. We too must pray prayers of supplication and thanksgiving. When we pray, we must ask for what we need and give God thanks in advance, knowing that our needs will be supplied according to God's riches in glory. We must pray without ceasing. We must take our concerns to the Lord in prayer. And we must be thankful. We must thank God for all things.

If you pray out of a thankful heart, you may be at it for a while. Thank God first for the joy of your salvation. Thank God that Jesus our Christ did not think it robbery to disrobe himself in heaven and come down as a babe in order to save us. What love! How can we not praise God? Then thank God for the grace and forgiveness you have experienced. There is great joy in knowing that no matter how we mess up, God loves us. "Joyful, joyful, Lord we adore thee." *Rejoice, and again I say, rejoice.*

In verse 7, Paul writes that the peace of God will protect their hearts and minds. God is a God of peace. God gives peace to those who trust God. Others should look at those of us who are Christians and marvel at our composure. Our neighbors should be able to see that even though we face adversaries, we do not wallow in fear. They should know that even though we walk through the swirling waters that could pull us into the depths of despair, our faith in God instead gives us joy that lifts us up and allows us to prevail. Our friends should watch us and know that we believe; we trust that God can turn it around, that God will work in our favor. I pray that when the world sees us, they will want what we have and will inquire how we could be at such peace even though the world seems to be falling down around us.

Remember the words of David in Psalm 24:9: "Lift up your heads, O ye gates; even lift them up, ye everlasting doors; and the King of glory shall come in." Who is this King of glory? The Lord of hosts, our God, is the king of glory.

God will keep us in perfect peace if we keep our minds on God. We stumble when we focus on the circumstances and lose sight of the creator, when we focus on the problem and lose sight of the provider, when we focus on the mess and miss the message, and when we depend on ourselves and diminish the defender. Peace comes when we depend on the Lord's strength and when we find joy in the Lord, when we remember that joy comes in the morning, that we possess the joy of our salvation, when we know that in Christ we have more than enough, and when we embrace the truth that joy comes not in being able to change our circumstances but in allowing God to change us.

Finally, in verse 8 of Philippians 4, Paul tells us that the only things worthy of our praise are those that are true and honest, just and pure, pleasing and commendable. And we know, as followers of Christ, that Jesus is the one that is true, the one that is honorable, the one that is just, the one that is pure, and the one that is pleasing and commendable. We can rejoice because we follow and serve a God of excellence, a God who is above and beyond all that is good.

The less often quoted last part of Niebuhr's Serenity Prayer is a fitting reminder of how we can have joy in spite of all we face:

Living one day at a time;
Enjoying one moment at a time;
Accepting hardships as the pathway to peace;
Taking, as He did, this sinful world
as it is, not as I would have it;
Trusting that He will make all things right
if I surrender to His Will;
That I may be reasonably happy in this life
and supremely happy with Him
Forever in the next. Amen.[4]

Rejoice, and again I say, rejoice.

Notes

1. Bobby McFerrin, "Don't Worry, Be Happy," 1988.
2. Reinhold Niebuhr, "The Serenity Prayer," 1943.
3. Shirley Caesar, "This Joy I Have."
4. Niebuhr, "The Serenity Prayer."

Chapter Twenty-Six

On Parenting: Love without Honor
(1 Thessalonians 2:7-13)

Erin James-Brown
2012 Recipient of the Addie Davis Award for Excellence in Preaching

I am not a very athletic person. I do not know if you can tell from my soft arms or extremely skinny calves, but I have never been much for sports. My hand-eye coordination is so bad that I have trouble correctly lifting a cup of water to my lips without spilling it, let alone throwing or catching a ball. My poor coordination plagued me throughout my childhood. After many failed attempts at T-ball, karate, and gymnastics, I tried one last time to overcome my gracelessness. At that time, the roller-skating rink was the coolest place that a fourth grader could hang out. Racing, video games, popsicles, and couples skate—magical things happened at the roller-skating rink. Every time my day care went to the skating rink, I dreamed of speeding past boys twice my size and sliding across the finish line with triumphantly blazing wheels. I wanted to be the best roller-skater ever.

So my mom signed me up for figure roller-skating. Now, figure roller-skating is not a very popular sport. It is kind of like ice figure skating with a lot less glamour, glitter, and chilly elegance. Plus, it is not very competitive. Only four or five people in the whole world are figure roller-skaters. This, of course, was the perfect sport for me.

Every Saturday morning, I put on my tasteful red skating skirt, along with bright white skates with matching gleaming wheels, and maneuvered out onto the rink. I watched as girls four or five years older moved like gazelles across the smooth surface, their muscular legs bulging with every stroke, propelling them faster as they prepared for jumps, spins, and graceful arm-dancing motions. In comparison, my stick-like legs heaved to lift the gargantuan skates and move across the floor. As time progressed, I gained more confidence with my abilities to glide on eight wheels underneath the glow of a disco ball. I learned to stop using a traditional toe stopper rather than smacking into dirty brown, carpeted walls. I could make figure eights backwards and forwards with ease. It seemed I had overcome my fear and inability to coordinate my body to do as I my brain commanded. Until . . . one highly anticipated Saturday morning.

That day I woke early with butterflies in my stomach. With difficulty, I pulled on my glossy tights and form-fitting skating uniform. When my parents and I arrived at the rink, there was a buzz in the air. It was competition day. Skaters from all over the surrounding area arrived to be judged according to their routines and abilities . . . so there were like five competitors there. As my turn approached, I skated out onto the rink to the cheers of my parents as they sat in a practically empty room. Still, I was nervous. As the music swelled, I began to display my limited knowledge of figure roller-skating dance by waving my arms around a bit and swizzling my feet left and right. I do not remember the routine or song to which I performed. All I remember is at the closing of the program I performed a single-legged spin. My heart leapt in my throat as my feet approached the exact spot on the floor where I should enter the rotation. As I swung my body into position, I prepared to maintain balance for several consecutive turns. However, before I could even get into position, I overcompensated, throwing my body into a hard right spin. My heavy skates slipped out from underneath my angular frame, carrying my skinny legs above me. My bony bottom crashed to the floor as my boyish haircut flew in my face. The music blared as the two audience members—my parents—loudly gasped. In mortification, I pulled myself up off the floor as best I could. My shaky legs could not twist back into a spin. Instead, I finished the rest of the routine, replaying in my mind scenes from the triumphal disgrace of the bobsled team from *Cool Runnings* in hopes that I still maintained a shred of my ten-year-old dignity. After the music concluded, I left the floor with my ears sunk between my shoulder blades. I was afraid to approach my coach, a mean-spirited taskmaster. I was even more embarrassed to approach my parents. I knew their hard work and money for lessons had not paid off as they had antici-pated. After the obvious awkwardness in my performance, along with the tumble, my parents probably knew their daughter would not be a figure rolling-skating star.

Just as parents hope for the prosperity and successfulness of their child, Paul in 1 Thessalonians 2 mentions parental support for both the people of Thessalonica and himself. Interestingly, he refers to the Thessalonians as a mother, caring for and nursing her young. The reason this reference is so interesting is that Paul needed some good care. Earlier, he had been run out of town, chased by people who despised him, and now he was physically and emotionally worn out. Despite that experience, Paul saw the Thessa-lonian Christians as a respite, an encouragement after a tiring journey. They nurtured and nestled the believers in their midst with tenderness in hopes of restoration. In return, Paul and his followers became like a parent to the Thessalonian church by "urging and encouraging" concerning a life worthy of God, who called them into God's kingdom and glory. Paul's mutual ref-erences to parental love, nurture, and support reveals the intimacy of his relationship with the Thessalonians. In the beginning the church provided physical nourishment for he and Silas. In turn, Paul offered spiritual guid-ance, bold encouragement, and a vision for the future joys among Christians of the church.

Parental care, as described by Paul, seems to be focused on preparing people for the coming of Christ through work and skill. He writes, "You remember our labor and toil, brothers and sisters; we worked night and day, so that we might not burden any of you while we proclaimed to you the gospel of God. You are witnesses, and God also, how pure, upright, and blameless our conduct was toward you believers" (1 Thess 2:9-10).

Later in chapter 4, he encourages his readers to lead quiet lives, working hard with their hands so that they are not dependent on others (4:11b-12). By warning and preparing the Thessalonians for the challenges ahead, Paul hopes to arm them with skills for the future. His love transcends the present moment in Thessalonica to remind them of his constant care in anticipated events. Much like Paul's experience, the Thessalonians could encounter dev-astating persecution, theological challenges, and internal dissention. Paul gives instructions in hopes of preventing wrestlings among the community, in hopes of helping them maintain a sense of peace and unity. However, is this a true parental image to follow? Are we to be like Paul, urging our chil-dren and fellow believers to practice and grow in talent in order to be successful individuals?

I do not read parenting books, but I once ran across an extremely moving article about parenting in the *New York Times*. Emily Rapp gave birth
to a beautiful baby boy whom she named Ronan or "little seal." After several
months of newborn baby bliss, Ronan was diagnosed with Tay-Sachs disease,
a rare, terminal illness that would kill him by his third birthday. At the
moment of diagnosis, Emily had to make a new choice about her parenting
style. Instead of taking Ronan to Mommy and Me swim lessons or baby
yoga practice, developing his body and mind for excellent function and assis-
tance in life skills, Emily realized her child would never take the SATs,
graduate from college, or start his own family. He would not have a job, a
favorite movie, or even utter his first word. Mothering suddenly became
much more difficult than what she had anticipated. How do you parent a
child who will die before you do? With the brevity of life looming over the
cradle, what parts of everyday events become important, hold significance,
and create dignity for a sweet baby slipping into a vegetable-like state? In
the article, Emily wrote,

> We never thought about how we might parent a child for whom there is
> no future . . . . We are not waiting for Ronan to make us proud. [But he]
> has given us a terrible freedom from expectations, a magical world where
> there are no goals, no prizes to win, no outcomes to monitor, discuss, com-
> pare . . . . The only task here is to love."[1]

Emily's words came as a response to other parenting books, which encourage
stringent methods of raising children toward successful adulthood. Gaining
thoughtful inspiration from her terminally ill child, Emily wrote about the
difficulty of loving children in the present without expectations of their
future: "Parenting, I've come to understand, is about loving my child
today."[2]

Traditional parenting naturally presumes a future in which the child
outlives the parent and ideally becomes successful, perhaps even achieves
something spectacular. Parents take on the responsibility for instructing their
children in hopes that they will flourish as adults. In turn, children obey
their parents, and in the end, every child grows up into a functional human
being. That is good parenting, right? According to Paul, do good parents
provide the guidance needed in order to produce victorious, upstanding
children of God? Or is there something more?

There are moments in our lives when we fall, when our flimsy bodies
will not carry us any further, and we need the comfort and guidance of a

nursing parent. Paul had reached a moment like that. He had exhausted his resources and energies by the time he approached Thessalonica. Wearily, he dragged himself, along with his disciples, into the city looking for work, companionship, and comfort. The Thessalonian Gentiles who listened and believed Paul's words about Jesus Christ took it upon themselves to provide tender care for the man and his followers. They worked alongside him, cheered him on through difficult situations, and remained loyal friends despite persecution. And Paul wrote of them, "We were gentle among you, like a nurse tenderly caring for her own children. So deeply do we care for you that we are determined to share with you not only the gospel of God but also our own selves, because you have become very dear to us" (1 Thess 2:11-12).

As the fellow believers of Thessalonica cared for Paul, so Paul grew to appreciate and love the generous nature of his friends in the city. In turn, the apostle sought to maintain a healthy relationship with his fellow Christians. He worked in order to support himself, without creating debts or exhibiting selfish laziness while he lived among them. The relationship went beyond mere words. The Christians with Paul shared their life's work, life's secrets, and life's passions with their friends. Their relationship blossomed under the ideas of understanding and acceptance.

My first figure roller-skating competition was my last figure roller-skating competition. After removing the white weights of disgrace from my scrawny ankles of shame, I sheepishly walked up to Mom and Dad. Because of my jerky movements out on the floor and my collapsed spin move, my mother and father packed up their dreams of a coordinated child. They would never attend basketball games, cheerleading camps, or dance recitals. They accepted the fact that their only child walked a little like Arnold Schwarzenegger in *The Terminator* and danced a lot like SpongeBob SquarePants. My parents settled for sitting through three-hour-long high school plays with poor British accents, making posters to elect Erin for student council, and driving long distances to debate tournaments filled with overdressed nerds in ill-fitting suits. But that day, as I approached my parents, sweaty with disappointing anxiety, my mom embraced me in a big hug and smiled brightly. "You were so brave," she said. "Even though you fell, you got right back up."

It turns out that in figure roller-skating, everyone receives a medal, even the ones who fall down. I pinned my prize onto my team sweatshirt and carried my heavy gym bag out of the rink. To my parents' relief, I quit figure roller-skating a few weeks later.

Paul's use of maternal and paternal imagery in 1 Thessalonians point us to the meaning of love. Love is not an investment in the future in which you hope to make a profit. Love is the gift of dignity and respect that a person deserves just because he or she is a human being. As Christians, we give of ourselves extravagantly in order to communicate the gospel message. Our goodness is not based on occupation, hobby, or skill. Our saintliness is part of who we are. We make our work and lives holy and communicate love through our words, actions, and attitudes. This does not mean we do not get angry, disappointed, or scared. In fact, it is just the opposite. By being truly ourselves, we display who God created us to be, and by embracing ourselves, we open up our souls to others, welcoming their true personhood to the table as well. We act as mother and father, loving and encouraging others. In addition, we have spiritual mothers and fathers of the faith who carry us along during difficult times. These saints, like Paul and the Thessalonians, inspire us to live with courage, making every day holy.

The love of spiritual parentage does not calculate success, does not find utter disappointment in failure, and does not plan for future expectation of fulfillment. Instead, the challenge and joy of spiritual parenting celebrates the love of the present—a present without honors or a rational reason to celebrate accomplishment.

Notes

1. Emily Rapp, "Notes from a Dragon Mom," *New York Times*, 15 October 2011.
2. Ibid.

Chapter Twenty-Seven

In Thanksgiving; Hope!
Molly Brummett

A New Vision
(Revelation 21:1-5)

Molly Brummett

*2013 Recipient of the Addie Davis
Award for Excellence in Preaching*

I was not an imaginative child. If I ever
played "make-believe," I wanted the "make-
believe" to have a purpose. Once, my friend Meredith and I created an
impressive elementary school underneath massive tents. We used chairs,
blankets, and sheets to pitch our enlightened educational institution. It was
one of the finest tents for learning that anyone had ever seen. Our aim was
to teach in order to enlighten our imaginary friends but also to grow ourselves. I vividly remember Meredith telling me, "This will help us one day
with our careers."

Meredith and I also created a make-believe television show—a spinoff
on *The Oprah Winfrey Show*. One day another friend came over so that she
could be a guest on our show. She started talking about her own Neverland,
a place where fairies and Barbies lined the streets and sang to her as she
skipped down the golden roads. I got *so mad*. I stomped my foot and yelled,
"Stop! That isn't real. Stop imagining such crazy things!"

The final book in the Bible, Revelation, is quite imaginative. The writer
casts Revelation in the form of a vision of things that must "soon take place."
The entire book is bizarre, with crazy, almost psychedelic imagery. Many
scholars call Revelation a "highly ambiguous and difficult" text. I am starting
to agree with them.

After all, the writer is a seer living on the island of Patmos, and there he
has a great revelation. And *this* revelation to "St. John, the Divine" takes
shape in the format of a letter from the exalted Christ to the seven churches
in Asia Minor. In the letter, churches are either encouraged or rebuked;

beasts and angels are woven throughout the narrative; and disturbing images seem to be part of every mention of women. In Revelation, God's acts of judgment are described in seven cycles to the seven churches. A tripped-out, dropping-acid pattern of eschatological resolution forms the basis of this entire work, and we say to our educated and enlightened selves, "This is *not* reality." And I am starting to think, "Why is preaching this now *my* reality?!"

But here we are, in this crazy, wildly imaginative text, engaging and engaged by this pinnacle moment that is recorded in chapter 21: "Then I saw a new heaven and a new earth, for the first heaven and the first earth had passed away, and the sea was no more. And I saw the holy city, the New Jerusalem, coming down out of heaven from God, prepared as a bride adorned for her husband" (vv. 1-2).

Proclamations resound: a new heaven, new earth; a holy city coming from heaven like a bride; a *new*, almost unrealistic vision. Yet these proclamations are in our Bible. These words are canonized. This is a vision . . . a hope . . . for *us* as God's people. We often skip over this hope of a new heaven and a new earth. We know that Revelation is apocalyptic in nature, so we often get scared and toss this work to the side. (Well, not all people toss it aside because there are plenty of freaky, scary judgment houses still going on in October each year.) But the apocalyptic theological perspective found in this text makes it easy to "categorize," "box up," and say, "Oh, that text is just about the end times, not about *our* time."

We justify our neglect of the text, saying that it does not matter in the here and now. We believe that a new heaven and a new earth will not take place in our lifetime. There is just too much evidence against the unfolding of a new heaven and a new earth. We find it almost impossible to imagine when news of violence and suffering flood our television sets. It is tough to think about a new hope when some of our brothers and sisters are blatantly denied civil rights. It is rough to dream about a new heaven and a new earth when racial discrimination still permeates our society. Keeping this apocalyptic text in the confines of "end time" literature is the easiest and most logical thing to do. Or so we think.

Have you ever seen an optical illusion painting? I am sure most of us have seen the image that is both an old woman and a young maiden. Or perhaps, like me, you sat in a psychology class and the professor pulled out an image that embodies both a saxophonist and a big head. When our eyes are first drawn to such paintings, we often can only see *one* of the images. For some of us, it is hard to ever see the other image. These illusions are visually perceived images that differ from objective reality. The information gathered by the eye is processed in the brain to give a perception that does not necessarily coincide with our initial understanding. We think that there is only one thing to see, and then, "BAM!" We are seeing something completely different! We have all had that "BAM" moment when viewing these illusions, that moment that shifts our way of seeing. What we thought was the *only* reality no longer computes. We think and see differently.

"See, the home of God is among mortals. God will dwell with them; they will be God's peoples, and God will be with them. God will wipe every tear from their eyes. Death will be no more; mourning and crying and pain will be no more, for the first things have passed away" (Revelation 21:3-4). Here, at this point in the text, is where the people of faith we call saints come in. I think they are called saints because they *see* differently. They have a new vision, and in their new vision is found hope. The saints realize that this "indwelling" of God—the One who created us, calls us, and sustains us—means that the old reality *no longer computes!*

In verse 3, we find the Greek word *skene*, which translates as tabernacle or "pitched tent." *Skene* is also found in John 1:14: "the Word became *flesh* and *dwelt among us!*" The saints "got" the connection.

Verses 3-4 in chapter 21 proclaim the eschatological exclamation of this entire Revelation of God, first to John at Patmos, then to the various saints, and now to us. God *dwells* with God's people. The saints fully comprehended the power in this proclamation for our world. They realized that dreaming, imagining, and living into the vision of a new heaven and a new earth is possible in the here and now because the Word has already become flesh and dwelt among us. God pitched a tent in this world through the Incarnation, and the saints are saints because they understood that truth. They believed that God called them to pitch a tent in this world next to God, and so they did!

This dwelling of God shifts our understanding of this inspired text. No longer is it merely an apocalyptic, futuristic, eschatological literary piece. It moves to the present. This dwelling must be lived into so that a new heaven and a new earth might dawn in creation for all of God's people. Here. Now.

God is already here, tabernacling with *us*, God's people. God's tent is pitched. But amid the busyness and stresses of our lives, we too often forget that reality of hope. The stresses of status quo, ever-achieving, middle-to-upperclass living mixed with the weight of injustice, discrimination, and radical evil keep us from fully realizing that God is here, dwelling, tabernacling, pitching tents already. Far too often, our dreams become enslaved by the stresses bearing down on us. We forget that we too are called as were the saints to pitch our tents, to live into the dream, so that a new heaven and a new earth breaks forth. Barbara Brown Taylor wrote of it this way:

> We are all dreamers, but dreamers have fallen upon hard times . . . . We belong to a people whose sense of reality is much more limited. We have been schooled in science and philosophy; we have learned to trust what we can handle and prove. We have been taught to think, not to dream, and we have lived long enough to watch many of our dreams die hard. Only saints and children still believe their dreams will come true. The rest of us are adults who know the difference between fact and fantasy.[1]

The key for us "fact not fantasy" folks sitting here today is to reach back to our saints. We must learn from them. We must understand that God's vision is not only an eschatological miracle. Human agency can and should be involved. The saints realized that. They were the human agents who, throughout history, were infused with the Spirit of new creation and who contributed and still contribute to the future reign of God. They pitched tents, despite the muck of the world, in the here and now.

For the saints' lives not to have been lived in vain, we must honor them by choosing to dream again. We must live into the *hope* of a new heaven and a new earth. We must learn to dream as they dreamed. We must pitch a tent in this world. We must learn to see as they saw. We must work at seeing both images within the optical illusions. We must realize that the reality as we know it does not have to be the *only* one. There is more than meets the eye. A new heaven and a new earth are not far away. "See, I am making all things new . . . . Write this, for these words are trustworthy and true" (Rev 21:5).

In order to see, in order to dream, in order to be about this new heaven and new earth, we must get out of our confined and preconceived visions of this world: How is it? How should it be? How do we think it will be? We must shift our eyes to realize that this revelatory text urges us to engage in a new vision.

This vision is not ours to build; it is the gift of God. Yet as gift, it does not call for passivity. It calls for action. The saints saw this gift; they acted upon it; and now we too are called to act. For you see, God indeed desires to make all things new. But by the grace of God, we are not puppets, and God is not our puppeteer. Therefore, we have the choice to respond to this gift of being about a new heaven and a new earth. The saints before us entered into the gift. They chose to respond boldly. They pitched tents all around. They chose to dream a dream that at times seemed crazy. Our saints dreamed:

from St. Francis of Assisi to Thomas Merton,
from Dorothy Day to Mother Teresa,
from St. Paul to Martin Luther,
from Teresa De Avila to Mary Oliver,
from Balthasar Hubmaier to Roger Williams,
from Mary Magdalene to Marian Wright Edelman
from Dietrich Bonhoeffer to Martin Luther King, Jr.

They *all* knew that a new heaven and a new earth did not have to mean "the end times." It could mean "the present time." They lived lives ushering in a new heaven and a new earth to our world. They knew and believed that God dwells with us. They chose to pitch a tent in this world next to God's tent. They knew they could dream a *dream* of a new heaven and a new earth because *God's* tent was right there beside theirs.

And as the saints pitched their tents, they joined God one tent over and sang,

Come let us dream God's dream again. Come let us dream. Though dreamers die the dream will live for we have yet our lives to give. Come let us dream God's dream again. Won't you join us, sister, friend, you are just what we need. Come let us dream God's dream again, brother, come on, too. We know it's daunting to dream again, to dream something anew. But come, let us dream God's dream again, for we shall not be alone. Though dreamers die, the dream will live, for the world will finally be made whole.[2]

I was not an imaginative child, but the song of the saints beckons me to think. Their song reminds me that we are called to imagine, to pitch tents, to dream.

Notes

1. Barbara Brown Taylor, *Gospel Medicine* (Cambridge MA: Cowley Publications, 1995) 114.

2. Adapted from John Middleton, "Come, Let Us Dream" (Nashville: United Methodist General Board of Discipleship, 2004).

The Preachers

Gwen Brown was the 2010 recipient of the Addie Davis Award for Outstanding Leadership in Pastoral Ministry. Gwen was the founding pastor of Cornerstone Church in Snellville, Georgia, a congregation that began as a Bible study meeting in her home in 2005. In 2007, Gwen left her job in the corporate world to enroll at McAfee School of Theology. Graduating in 2010, Gwen spent her time teaching spiritual formation as an adjunct professor at McAfee, serving on the Baptist Women in Ministry leadership team, and serving as a member of the Cooperative Baptist Fellowship of Georgia's Coordinating Council. Sadly, Gwen died on August 27, 2013, leaving behind her husband, Charles, her two daughters, Robin and Candice Briggs, and a host of family and friends who continue to miss her greatly.

Erin James-Brown was the 2012 recipient of the Addie Davis Award for Excellence in Preaching. A graduate of Logsdon Theological Seminary, Abilene, Texas, Erin currently works as a hospital chaplain by day at Texas Health Harris Methodist Hospital in Fort Worth, Texas, and serves as a youth and children's minister by night. Her schedule is packed with care to those in crisis, pastoral counseling, retelling Bible stories around a semicircle of smiling, never bored young faces, and painting with watercolors. Erin especially enjoys running along the Trinity River with her oversized lab, Walter, and her handsome husband, Joel.

Molly Brummett was the 2013 recipient of the Addie Davis Award for Excellence in Preaching. Molly hails from Jefferson City, Tennessee, but now calls Winston-Salem, North Carolina, home. A graduate of Carson-Newman University and Wake Forest University School of Divinity, she serves as minister of youth and community at Knollwood Baptist Church. Molly loves strong coffee, authentic conversations, walks in the woods, and laughter among friends.

Caroline Lawson Dean was the 2008 recipient of the Addie Davis Award for Outstanding Leadership in Pastoral Ministry. Since 2009, she has served as associate pastor of adult and youth faith formation at Christ Church, Summit, New Jersey. Caroline is a graduate of the University of Richmond, where she studied Religion and Psychology, and she received her Master of Divinity degree from Duke Divinity School. Along with her husband, Brantley, Caroline loves being outside with their dog, Tex. She also enjoys dabbling in guitar and art journaling as well as snuggling with her nieces and nephews.

Bailey Nelson Edwards was the 2008 recipient of the Addie Davis Award for Excellence in Preaching. Bailey has served on the pastoral staff of congregations throughout the Southeast, most recently as pastor in North Carolina. She is a graduate of Furman University and McAfee School of Theology. Bailey loves the creative arts, finding immense joy in her musical endeavors as a violinist and vocalist. She has also discovered a talent for painting that has given new expression to her life and faith. Bailey's husband, Justin, is a hospice chaplain. They have one son, Aidan, who provides endless wild and wonderful sermon illustrations.

Griselda Escobar was the 2011 recipient of the Addie Davis Award for Outstanding Leadership in Pastoral Ministry. Griselda is a chaplain at Christus-Spohn South Hospital in Corpus Christi, Texas. A graduate of Baptist University of the Americas in San Antonio, and Logsdon Theological Seminary in Abilene, she completed Clinical Pastoral Education at Trinity Mother Frances Hospital in Tyler. Griselda is married to Allan, and they have a son, Elijah. Their family enjoys walks on the beach and watching the beauty of the sky, and for Griselda, the calm of living near the ocean has brought her much joy and given her opportunities for meditation and rest.

Angela Fields was the 2012 recipient of the Addie Davis Award for Outstanding Leadership in Pastoral Ministry. Angela is a writer and speaker. Her recent children's book, *I'm Perfectly Different,* led to the creation of a nonprofit organization of the same name, which allows her to continue her focus on issues of health care, socioeconomic challenges, and interpersonal relationships and community building. A graduate of McAfee School of Theology, Angela spends her free time with friends and family and enjoys shopping and eating at her favorite restaurants.

Nicole Finkelstein-Blair was the 2001 recipient of the Addie Davis Award for Excellence in Preaching. She is a graduate of Samford University in Birmingham, Alabama, and Central Baptist Theological Seminary in Shawnee, Kansas. Since her ordination in 2001, Nicole has been a US Navy spouse, participating in churches everywhere her family has been stationed (five states and the United Kingdom so far), and eagerly accepting pulpit-supply invitations. She and her husband, Scott, a Navy chaplain, and their two sons recently relocated from San Antonio, Texas, to Beaufort, South Carolina.

Karen Hatcher was the 2010 recipient of the Addie Davis Award for Excellence in Preaching. A former teacher turned preacher, Karen, or Kam as her friends call her, serves with A Christian Ministry in the National Parks (ACMNP) in the Shenandoah National Park in Virginia. She conducts weekly worship and offers pastoral care to employees and visitors. A graduate of the Baptist Theological Seminary at Richmond and a "retiree" from Chesterfield County Public Schools, Kam loves writing, dancing, learning foreign languages, and connecting with far-flung family and friends. Also an avid hiker, she has walked the Galician portion of the ancient Camino de Santiago pilgrimage route in Spain.

LeAnn Gunter Johns was the 2004 recipient of the Addie Davis Award for Excellence in Preaching. A graduate of the University of West Florida and McAfee School of Theology, LeAnn has served as pastor of St. Clare Baptist Church, Macon, Georgia, and New Community Church in San Jose, California. She was also on the pastoral staff at Peachtree Baptist Church in Atlanta. Along with Pam Durso, LeAnn is the co-editor of *The World Waits for You: Celebrating the 50th Ordination Anniversary of Addie Davis*. She is married to Barry, a physician, and they have two sons, Parker and Patrick, and a sweet dog, Jovi.

Andrea Dellinger Jones was the 2002 recipient of the Addie Davis Award for Excellence in Preaching. Since 2008, Andrea has served as the pastor of Millbrook Baptist Church in Raleigh, North Carolina. She also teaches as an adjunct professor at Duke Divinity School. A graduate of Rhodes College, Andrea also earned her Master of Divinity degree from McAfee School of Theology and her Doctor of Ministry degree from Baptist Theological Seminary at Richmond. She and her husband, Brent, are still reeling with giddy delight over their new daughter, Anne Elyse Avila Jones.

Martha Kearse was the 2005 recipient of the Addie Davis Award for Excellence in Preaching. Since 2001, Martha has served as associate pastor at St. John's Baptist Church in Charlotte, North Carolina. But ministry is her second career. She began her professional life as a high school English teacher. A graduate of Gardner-Webb University's School of Divinity, Martha is married to Henry (Monty), and they have three children, Mattie, Conner, and Anna. A native of Charlottesville, Virginia, Martha is a lover of the mountains and visits them whenever she can. She also loves reading, writing, and hearing her children singing while they do the dishes (they sing well but do dishes poorly).

Veronice Miles was the 1999 recipient of the Addie Davis Award for Excellence in Preaching. She is the Ruby Pardue and Shelmer D. Blackburn Assistant Professor of Homiletics and Christian Education at Wake Forest University School of Divinity, Winston-Salem, North Carolina. Veronice earned her Bachelor of Arts and Master of Education degrees from the University of Florida and completed her Master of Divinity degree at Candler School of Theology in Atlanta. She then earned a PhD from Emory University. Author of numerous articles, she is currently writing a book with the working title of *Ain't Gonna Study War No More: Young Black Women and the Audacity to Live with Hope.* In addition to her academic commitments, Veronice serves as a minister at her church in Winston-Salem.

Heather Mustain was the 2013 recipient of the Addie Davis Award for Outstanding Leadership in Pastoral Ministry. A 2013 graduate of the George W. Truett Theological Seminary, Heather earned both the Master of Divinity and the Master of Social Work degrees. She now serves at Wilshire Baptist Church in Dallas, Texas, as minister of missions. She loves walking around White Rock Lake with her husband, Chad, and their five-year-old Boston terrier, Maeby.

Teresa Pugh was the 2005 recipient of the Addie Davis Award for Outstanding Leadership in Pastoral Ministry. Since 2010, Teresa has been pastor of Trinity Community Church in Hampton, Georgia. She previously served as Christian education and youth pastor of the Greater Piney Grove Baptist Church, Atlanta, and youth pastor of Fountain of Faith Missionary Baptist Church, Riverdale, Georgia. Teresa is founder and CEO of Bread Basket Ministries, Inc., and project coordinator for Bread Basket Thanksgiving. She pursued a Master of Science degree in public administration at Columbus University and earned a Master of Divinity degree from McAfee School of Theology. Her loves are traveling, reading, and most of all, giving.

Kimberly Schmitt Holman was the 2000 recipient of the Addie Davis Award for Excellence in Preaching. Kim currently works as staff chaplain and SIT (supervisor in training) at Piedmont Fayette Hospital, Fayetteville, Georgia. She has served as a pastor, associate pastor, and youth minister in several churches in North Carolina and Georgia. A graduate of Gardner-Webb University and McAfee School of Theology, Kim is wife to Mike and mother to Jacob. She loves spending time with her family and friends and finds peace and joy in nature. An avid reader, Kim also enjoying singing and playing music.

Kyndall Rae Rothaus was the 2011 recipient of the Addie Davis Award for Excellence in Preaching. Kyndall is a preacher, poet, liturgist and writer who pastors Covenant Baptist Church in San Antonio, Texas. A graduate of Southern Nazarene University, Bethany, Oklahoma, and the George W. Truett Theological Seminary, Waco, Texas, Kyndall has a passion for the spoken word, soulful creativity, and authentic transparency; words and nature are her constant source of inspiration. Her first book, *Preacher Breath*, will be published by Smyth & Helwys Books in 2014.

Shelley Hasty Woodruff was the 2007 recipient of the Addie Davis Award for Excellence in Preaching. A graduate of Furman University and McAfee School of Theology, she also has earned a Master of Theology degree in Homiletics from Columbia Theological Seminary in Decatur, Georgia, and is now completing a Doctor of Theology degree in Homiletics at Duke Divinity School. Shelley previously served as college and single adult minister at Wieuca Road Baptist Church in Atlanta. Now living in Durham, North Carolina, with her husband, Josh, and their daughter, Lottie, Shelley finds joy in coaching new ministers in the craft of preaching and marveling at the way a one-year-old brain sees the world.

Appendix

Addie Davis Award Recipients
1998-2014

1998: Kelly Bazemore, Tammy Condrey, Jennifer L. Dundas, Joy Heaton, Jana Stewart Kinnersley, Gloria Jean Ortega, Rachel A. Stephen

1999: Veronice Miles (preaching) and Virginia Dempsey (pastoral leadership)

2000: Kimberly L. Hardegree (preaching) and Ellen Holden DiGiosia (pastoral leadership)

2001: Nicole Finkelstein-Blair (preaching)

2002: Andrea Dellinger Jones (preaching) and Belinda Creighton-Smith (pastoral leadership)

2003: Susan Burnette (preaching) and Shirley Ramsey Luckadoo (pastoral leadership)

2004: LeAnn Gunter (preaching) and Holly Sprink (pastoral leadership)

2005: Martha Kearse (preaching) and Teresa Pugh (pastoral leadership)

2006: Stacy Cochran (preaching) and Debra Anne Carter (pastoral leadership)

2007: Shelley Hasty Woodruff (preaching) and Renee Kenley (pastoral leadership)

2008: Bailey Edwards Nelson (preaching) and Caroline Lawson (pastoral leadership)

2009: Marquette Bugg (preaching) and Tammy Jackson Gill (pastoral leadership)

2010: Karen Hatcher (preaching) and Gwen Brown (pastoral leadership)

2011: Kyndall Rothaus (preaching) and Griselda Escobar (pastoral leadership)

2012: Erin James-Brown (preaching) and Angela Fields (pastoral leadership)

2013: Molly Brummett (preaching) and Heather Mustain (pastoral leadership)

2014: Racquel Gill (preaching) and Erica Evans Whitaker (pastoral leadership)

INSTALLATION SERVICE

for the

Reverend Addie E. Davis

as minister of

The Second Baptist Church

Taunton Avenue at Walnut Street
East Providence, Rhode Island

SUNDAY SEPTEMBER 24, 1972 — 7:00 P.M.

++

Order of Service

ORGAN PRELUDE Hornpipe and Air from *"Water Music Suite"* *Handel*

*PROCESSIONAL HYMN *When I Survey The Wondrous Cross*   228

*INVOCATION AND LORD'S PRAYER   Mr. Dexter W. Smith

SCRIPTURE EPHESIANS 4:1-16   Mrs. Doris Berry

ANTHEM *Blessed Are They That Dwell In Thy House*   Chancel Choir

SERVICE OF INSTALLATION   Mr. Kenneth S. Wilder

> *Mr. Wilder:* In accordance with the belief of our Baptist Churches
> we sought the guidance of God in choosing a new minister
> for our church. After prayerful deliberation and due counsel
> we have been led to choose the Rev. Addie E. Davis as our
> pastor. We are met here this evening to install her as our
> spiritual leader and to pledge her our support and coopera-
> tion. I invite you, my fellow members and friends of the
> church to rise and join me in this act of installation.

> *Congregation:* We, the members of the Second Baptist Church
> do hereby install the Rev. Addie E. Davis as minister of this
> church. We solemnly pledge to walk with her in unity of
> spirit, in the bond of peace, and in all ways of God known to
> us or to be made known unto us. We furthermore pledge
> such faithfulness in worship and work, and such loyalty to
> Christ and His Church in stewardship of our talents and pos-
> sessions, as will advance the Kingdom of God in our church
> and in our community.

++

▶+++

*Prayer of Installation   Mr. Gordon D. Crocker

*Hymn *O Jesus, I Have Promised*   308

Charge to Church   Rev. W. Eugene Motter

Charge to Pastor   Rev. Robert S. Carlson

GREETINGS

Rhode Island State Council of Churches — Rev. James M. Webb
Rhode Island Baptist State Convention — Rev. W. Eugene Motter
East Providence Ministers' Association — Rev. Glenn H. Payne

*Recessional Hymn *Living For Jesus A Life That Is True*   304

*The Benediction   The Rev. Addie E. Davis

Organ Postlude *Postlude in G Major*   Handel

*The congregation standing.

————————◆————————

The ushers will dismiss the congregation by rows to leave by the side
entrance for the reception, which will follow in the Johnson Memorial
Room.

▶+++

Those Participating in the Service

Mr. Dexter W. Smith — *Chairman, Diaconate Board*

Mrs. Doris Berry — *Chairman, Board of Deaconesses*

Mr. Kenneth S. Wilder — *Moderator, Second Baptist Church*

Mr. Gordon D. Crocker — *Former Interim Pastor And Life Deacon Second Baptist Church*

Rev. W. Eugene Motter — *Executive Secretary, Rhode Island Baptist State Convention*

Rev. Robert S. Carlson — *Former Interim Pastor, Second Baptist Church*

Rev. James M. Webb—*General Secretary, Rhode Island State Council of Churches*

Rev. Glenn H. Payne — *Pastor, First Baptist Church of East Providence*

Mrs. Janice Gammage — *Organist*

Pulpit Commttee

Kenneth S. Wilder, *Chairman*

Mrs. Dorothy Horton

Mrs. Kenneth S. Wilder

Mr. Dexter W. Smith

Mr. Gerald Schloesser

Mr. Austin Butterworth

Mr. Albert W. Berry

Other available titles from

#Connect
Reaching Youth Across the Digital Divide

Brian Foreman

Reaching our youth across the digital divide is a struggle for parents, ministers, and other adults who work with Generation Z—today's teenagers. *#Connect* leads readers into the technological landscape, encourages conversations with teenagers, and reminds us all to be the presence of Christ in every facet of our lives.   *978-1-57312-693-9 120 pages/pb* **$13.00**

1 Corinthians (Smyth & Helwys Annual Bible Study series)
Growing through Diversity

Don & Anita Flowers

Don and Anita Flowers present this comprehensive study of 1 Corinthians, filled with scholarly insight and dealing with such varied topics as marriage and sexuality, spiritual gifts and love, and diversity and unity. The authors examine Paul's relationship with the church in Corinth as well as the culture of that city to give context to topics that can seem far removed from Christian life today.   *Teaching Guide 978-1-57312-701-1 122 pages/pb* **$14.00**

Study Guide 978-1-57312-705-9 52 pages/pb **$6.00**

Beyond the American Dream
Millard Fuller

In 1968, Millard finished the story of his journey from pauper to millionaire to home builder. His wife, Linda, occasionally would ask him about getting it published, but Millard would reply, "Not now. I'm too busy." This is that story.   *978-1-57312-563-5 272 pages/pb* **$20.00**

Blissful Affliction
The Ministry and Misery of Writing

Judson Edwards

Edwards draws from more than forty years of writing experience to explore why we use the written word to change lives and how to improve the writing craft.   *978-1-57312-594-9 144 pages/pb* **$15.00**

To order call **1-800-747-3016** or visit **www.helwys.com**

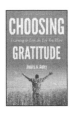

Choosing Gratitude
Learning to Love the Life You Have

James A. Autry

Autry reminds us that gratitude is a choice, a spiritual—not social—process. He suggests that if we cultivate gratitude as a way of being, we may not change the world and its ills, but we can change our response to the world. If we fill our lives with moments of gratitude, we will indeed love the life we have. *978-1-57312-614-4 144 pages/pb **$15.00***

Choosing Gratitude 365 Days a Year
Your Daily Guide to Grateful Living

James A. Autry and Sally J. Pederson

Filled with quotes, poems, and the inspired voices of both Pederson and Autry, in a society consumed by fears of not having "enough"—money, possessions, security, and so on—this book suggests that if we cultivate gratitude as a way of being, we may not change the world and its ills, but we can change our response to the world. *978-1-57312-689-2 210 pages/pb **$18.00***

Contextualizing the Gospel
A Homiletic Commentary on 1 Corinthians

Brian L. Harbour

Harbour examines every part of Paul's letter, providing a rich resource for those who want to struggle with the difficult texts as well as the simple texts, who want to know how God's word—all of it—intersects with their lives today. *978-1-57312-589-5 240 pages/pb **$19.00***

Dance Lessons
Moving to the Beat of God's Heart

Jeanie Miley

Miley shares her joys and struggles a she learns to "dance" with the Spirit of the Living God. *978-1-57312-622-9 240 pages/pb **$19.00***

A Divine Duet
Ministry and Motherhood

Alicia Davis Porterfield, ed.

Each essay in this inspiring collection is as different as the mother-minister who wrote it, from theologians to chaplains, inner-city ministers to rural-poverty ministers, youth pastors to preachers, mothers who have adopted, birthed, and done both.

*978-1-57312-676-2 146 pages/pb **$16.00***

The Enoch Factor
The Sacred Art of Knowing God
Steve McSwain

The Enoch Factor is a persuasive argument for a more enlightened religious dialogue in America, one that affirms the goals of all religions—guiding followers in self-awareness, finding serenity and happiness, and discovering what the author describes as "the sacred art of knowing God." *978-1-57312-556-7 256 pages/pb* **$21.00**

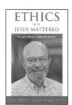

Ethics as if Jesus Mattered
Essays in Honor of Glen H. Stassen
Rick Axtell, Michelle Tooley, Michael L. Westmoreland-White, eds.

Ethics as if Jesus Mattered will introduce Stassen's work to a new generation, advance dialogue and debate in Christian ethics, and inspire more faithful discipleship just as it honors one whom the contributors consider a mentor. *978-1-57312-695-3 234 pages/pb* **$18.00**

Healing Our Hurts
Coping with Difficult Emotions
Daniel Bagby

In *Healing Our Hurts*, Daniel Bagby identifies and explains all the dynamics at play in these complex emotions. Offering practical biblical insights to these feelings, he interprets faith-based responses to separate overly religious piety from true, natural human emotion. This book helps us learn how to deal with life's difficult emotions in a redemptive and responsible way. *978-1-57312-613-7 144 pages/pb* **$15.00**

Help! I Teach Youth Sunday School
Brian Foreman, Bo Prosser, and David Woody

Real-life stories are mingled with information on Youth and their culture, common myths about Sunday School, a new way of preparing the Sunday school lesson, creative teaching ideas, ways to think about growing a class, and how to reach out for new members and reach in to old members. *1-57312-427-3 128 pages/pb* **$14.0**

Hope for the Thinking Christian
Seeking a Path of Faith through Everyday Life
Stephen Reese

Readers who want to confront their faith more directly, to think it through and be open to God in an individual, authentic, spiritual encounter will find a resonant voice in Stephen Reese.

978-1-57312-553-6 160 pages/pb **$16.00**

To order call **1-800-747-3016** or visit **www.helwys.com**

A Hungry Soul Desperate to Taste God's Grace
Honest Prayers for Life
Charles Qualls

Part of how we *see* God is determined by how we *listen* to God. There is so much noise and movement in the world that competes with images of God. This noise would drown out God's beckoning voice and distract us. Charles Qualls's newest book offers readers prayers for that journey toward the meaning and mystery of God.   *978-1-57312-648-9 152 pages/pb* **$14.00**

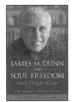

James M. Dunn and Soul Freedom
Aaron Douglas Weaver

James Milton Dunn, over the last fifty years, has been the most aggressive Baptist proponent for religious liberty in the United States. Soul freedom—voluntary, uncoerced faith and an unfettered individual conscience before God—is the basis of his understanding of church-state separation and the historic Baptist basis of religious liberty.   *978-1-57312-590-1 224 pages/pb* **$18.00**

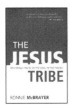

The Jesus Tribe
Following Christ in the Land of the Empire
Ronnie McBrayer

The Jesus Tribe fleshes out the implications, possibilities, contradictions, and complexities of what it means to live within the Jesus Tribe and in the shadow of the American Empire.

978-1-57312-592-5 208 pages/pb **$17.00**

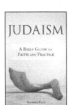

Judaism
A Brief Guide to Faith and Practice
Sharon Pace

Sharon Pace's newest book is a sensitive and comprehensive introduction to Judaism. What is it like to be born into the Jewish community? How does belief in the One God and a universal morality shape the way in which Jews see the world? How does one find meaning in life and the courage to endure suffering? How does one mark joy and forge community ties?   *978-1-57312-644-1 144 pages/pb* **$16.00**

Lessons from the Cloth 2
501 More One Minute Motivators for Leaders
Bo Prosser and Charles Qualls

As the force that drives organizations to accomplishment, leadership is at a crucial point in churches, corporations, families, and almost every arena of life. In this follow-up to their first volume, Prosser and Qualls will inspire you to keep growing in your leadership career.

978-1-57312-665-6 152 pages/pb **$11.00**

To order call **1-800-747-3016** or visit **www.helwys.com**

Let Me More of Their Beauty See
Reading Familiar Verses in Context

Diane G. Chen

Let Me More of Their Beauty See offers eight examples of how attention to the historical and literary settings can safeguard against taking a text out of context, bring out its transforming power in greater dimension, and help us apply Scripture appropriately in our daily lives.

978-1-57312-564-2 160 pages/pb **$17.00**

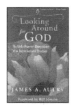

Looking Around for God
The Strangely Reverent Observations of an Unconventional Christian

James A. Autry

Looking Around for God, Autry's tenth book, is in many ways his most personal. In it he considers his unique life of faith and belief in God. Autry is a former Fortune 500 executive, author, poet, and consultant whose work has had a significant influence on leadership thinking.

978-157312-484-3 144 pages/pb **$16.00**

Making the Timeless Word Timely
A Primer for Preachers

Michael B. Brown

Michael Brown writes, "There is a simple formula for sermon preparation that creates messages that apply and engage whether your parish is rural or urban, young or old, rich or poor, five thousand members or fifty." The other part of the task, of course, involves being creative and insightful enough to know how to take the general formula for sermon preparation and make it particular in its impact on a specific congregation. Brown guides the reader through the formula and the skills to employ it with excellence and integrity.

978-1-57312-578-9 160 pages/pb **$16.00**

Meeting Jesus Today
For the Cautious, the Curious, and the Committed

Jeanie Miley

Meeting Jesus Today, ideal for both individual study and small groups, is intended to be used as a workbook. It is designed to move readers from studying the Scriptures and ideas within the chapters to recording their journey with the Living Christ.

978-1-57312-677-9 320 pages/pb **$19.00**

To order call **1-800-747-3016** or visit **www.helwys.com**

The Ministry Life
101 Tips for New Ministers
John Killinger

Sharing years of wisdom from more than fifty years in ministry and teaching, *The Ministry Life: 101 Tips for New Ministers* by John Killinger is filled with practical advice and wisdom for a minister's day-to-day tasks as well as advice on intellectual and spiritual habits to keep ministers of any age healthy and fulfilled. *978-1-57312-662-5 244 pages/pb* **$19.00**

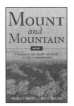

Mount and Mountain
Vol. 1: A Reverend and a Rabbi Talk About the Ten Commandments
Rami Shapiro and Michael Smith

Mount and Mountain represents the first half of an interfaith dialogue—a dialogue that neither preaches nor placates but challenges its participants to work both singly and together in the task of reinterpreting sacred texts. Mike and Rami discuss the nature of divinity, the power of faith, the beauty of myth and story, the necessity of doubt, the achievements, failings, and future of religion, and, above all, the struggle to live ethically and in harmony with the way of God. *978-1-57312-612-0 144 pages/pb* **$15.00**

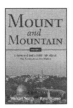

Mount and Mountain
Vol. 2: A Reverend and a Rabbi Talk About the Sermon on the Mount
Rami Shapiro and Michael Smith

This book, focused on the Sermon on the Mount, represents the second half of Mike and Rami's dialogue. In it, Mike and Rami explore the text of Jesus' sermon cooperatively, contributing perspectives drawn from their lives and religious traditions and seeking moments of illumination. *978-1-57312-654-0 254 pages/pb* **$19.00**

Overcoming Adolescence
Growing Beyond Childhood into Maturity
Marion D. Aldridge

In *Overcoming Adolescence*, Marion D. Aldridge poses questions for adults of all ages to consider. His challenge to readers is one he has personally worked to confront: to grow up *all the way*—mentally, physically, academically, socially, emotionally, and spiritually. The key involves not only knowing how to work through the process but also how to recognize what may be contributing to our perpetual adolescence.

978-1-57312-577-2 156 pages/pb **$17.00**

To order call **1-800-747-3016** or visit **www.helwys.com**

Psychic Pancakes & Communion Pizza
More Musings and Mutterings of a Church Misfit
Bert Montgomery

Psychic Pancakes & Communion Pizza is Bert Montgomery's highly anticipated follow-up to *Elvis, Willie, Jesus & Me* and contains further reflections on music, film, culture, life, and finding Jesus in the midst of it all. *978-1-57312-578-9 160 pages/pb* **$16.00**

Quiet Faith
An Introvert's Guide to Spiritual Survival
Judson Edwards

In eight finely crafted chapters, Edwards looks at key issues like evangelism, interpreting the Bible, dealing with doubt, and surviving the church from the perspective of a confirmed, but sometimes reluctant, introvert. In the process, he offers some provocative insights that introverts will find helpful and reassuring. *978-1-57312-681-6 144 pages/pb* **$15.00**

Reading Ezekiel (Reading the Old Testament series)
A Literary and Theological Commentary
Marvin A. Sweeney

The book of Ezekiel points to the return of YHWH to the holy temple at the center of a reconstituted Israel and creation at large. As such, the book of Ezekiel portrays the purging of Jerusalem, the Temple, and the people, to reconstitute them as part of a new creation at the conclusion of the book. With Jerusalem, the Temple, and the people so purged, YHWH stands once again in the holy center of the created world.

978-1-57312-658-8 264 pages/pb **$22.00**

Reading Hosea–Micah
(Reading the Old Testament series)
A Literary and Theological Commentary
Terence E. Fretheim

Terence E. Fretheim explores themes of indictment, judgment, and salvation in Hosea–Micah. The indictment against the people of God especially involves issues of idolatry, as well as abuse of the poor and needy. The effects of such behaviors are often horrendous in their severity. While God is often the subject of such judgments, the consequences, like fruit, grow out of the deed itself. *978-1-57312-687-8 224 pages/pb* **$22.00**

To order call **1-800-747-3016** or visit **www.helwys.com**

Reading Samuel (Reading the Old Testament series)
A Literary and Theological Commentary
Johanna W. H. van Wijk-Bos

Interpreted masterfully by preeminent Old Testament scholar Johanna W. H. van Wijk-Bos, the story of Samuel touches on a vast array of subjects that make up the rich fabric of human life. The reader gains an inside look at leadership, royal intrigue, military campaigns, occult practices, and the significance of religious objects of veneration.

978-1-57312-607-6 272 pages/pb **$22.00**

Sessions with Genesis (Session Bible Studies series)
The Story Begins
Tony W. Cartledge

Immersing us in the book of Genesis, Tony W. Cartledge examines both its major stories and the smaller cycles of hope and failure, of promise and judgment. Genesis introduces these themes of divine faithfulness and human failure in unmistakable terms, tracing Israel's beginning to the creation of the world and professing a belief that Israel's particular history had universal significance.

978-1-57312-636-6 144 pages/pb **$14.00**

Sessions with Revelation (Session Bible Studies series)
The Final Days of Evil
David Sapp

David Sapp's careful guide through Revelation demonstrates that it is a letter of hope for believers; it is less about the last days of history than it is about the last days of evil. Without eliminating its mystery, Sapp unlocks Revelation's central truths so that its relevance becomes clear.

978-1-57312-706-6 166 pages/pb **$14.00**

Silver Linings
My Life Before and After *Challenger 7*
June Scobee Rodgers

We know the public story of *Challenger 7*'s tragic destruction. That day, June's life took a new direction that ultimately led to the creation of the Challenger Center and to new life and new love. Her story of Christian faith and triumph over adversity will inspire readers of every age.

978-1-57312-570-3 352 pages/hc **$28.00**

978-1-57312-694-6 352 pages/pb **$18.00**

To order call **1-800-747-3016** or visit **www.helwys.com**

Spacious
Exploring Faith and Place
Holly Sprink

Exploring where we are and why that matters to God is an ongoing process. If we are present and attentive, God creatively and continuously widens our view of the world. *978-1-57312-649-6 156 pages/pb* **$16.00**

The Teaching Church
Congregation as Mentor
Christopher M. Hamlin / Sarah Jackson Shelton

Collected in *The Teaching Church: Congregation as Mentor* are the stories of the pastors who shared how congregations have shaped, nurtured, and, sometimes, broken their resolve to be faithful servants of God. *978-1-57312-682-3 112 pages/pb* **$13.00**

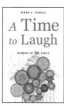

A Time to Laugh
Humor in the Bible
Mark E. Biddle

An extension of his well-loved seminary course on humor in the Bible, *A Time to Laugh* draws on Mark E. Biddle's command of Hebrew language and cultural subtleties to explore the ways humor was intentionally incorporated into Scripture. With characteristic liveliness, Biddle guides the reader through the stories of six biblical characters who did rather unexpected things. *978-1-57312-683-0 164 pages/pb* **$14.00**

This Is What a Preacher Looks Like
Sermons by Baptist Women in Ministry
Pamela Durso, ed.

In this collection of sermons by thirty-six Baptist women, their voices are soft and loud, prophetic and pastoral, humorous and sincere. They are African American, Asian, Latina, and Caucasian. They are sisters, wives, mothers, grandmothers, aunts, and friends.

978-1-57312-554-3 144 pages/pb **$18.00**

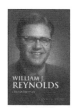

William J. Reynolds
Church Musician
David W. Music

William J. Reynolds is renowned among Baptist musicians, music ministers, song leaders, and hymnody students. In eminently readable style, David W. Music's comprehensive biography describes Reynolds's family and educational background, his career as a minister of music, denominational leader, and seminary professor. *978-1-57312-690-8 358 pages/pb* **$23.00**

To order call **1-800-747-3016** or visit **www.helwys.com**

Clarence Jordan's

COTTON PATCH

Gospel

The
Complete
Collection

The Cotton Patch Gospel, by Koinonia Farm founder Clarence Jordan, recasts the stories of Jesus and the letters of the New Testament into the language and culture of the mid-twentieth-century South. Born out of the civil rights struggle, these now-classic translations of much of the New Testament bring the far-away places of Scripture closer to home: Gainesville, Selma, Birmingham, Atlanta, Washington D.C.

Hardback • 448 pages

Retail ~~50.00~~ **• Your Price 45.00**

More than a translation, *The Cotton Patch Gospel* continues to make clear the startling relevance of Scripture for today. Now for the first time collected in a single, hardcover volume, this edition comes complete with a new Introduction by President Jimmy Carter, a Foreword by Will D. Campbell, and an Afterword by Tony Campolo. Smyth & Helwys Publishing is proud to help reintroduce these seminal works of Clarence Jordan to a new generation of believers, in an edition that can be passed down to generations still to come.

To order call **1-800-747-3016**
or visit **www.helwys.com**

11818814R00127

Made in the USA
San Bernardino, CA
01 June 2014